"Compelling, challenging, and entertaining, this ⟨...⟩
tive guide on how to build and lead high-trust tea⟨...⟩
—**The Honorable Bob Schaffer,** U.S. House of R⟨...⟩
businessm⟨...⟩

"In typical Peak Solutions fashion, the wisdom in these pages is edgy yet simple, straightforward, and proven. Take Richard's advice to heart to help you build the courage you need to give trust to others."
—**Rick Copeland,** VP of Human Resources, Restaurant Technologies, Inc.

"As a pastor I lead teams and work with people everyday. It is vital that relationships are healthy and strong. The principles in *Trustology* are pillars of successful relationships. This is a refreshing and wisdom-filled approach to a key issue in life. I love the relevance, intelligence and applicability of Richard's message. *Trustology* is a must read."
—**Aaron Stern,** pastor, Mill City Church, and author of *What's Your Secret?*

"A powerful analysis of what makes teams work effectively. This new way of looking at trust is a must-read for any leader that has come to grips with the fact that they must win the war on relationships to be successful at work."
—**Keith Hesterberg,** president and CEO, Fresno-Madera Farm Credit

"*Trustology* is full of unconventional wisdom and clear examples of how to succeed in our low-trust world. No MBA jargon or consultant-speak, and, best of all, practical advice we can all use."
—**Kevin Brinkman,** cofounder and president, Brinkman Partners

"As I've reviewed the relationships I have experienced over the past forty-plus years as a military officer, public school teacher, principal, and leadership consultant, I would have to say that Richard Fagerlin is precisely on target with his insight that trust is the essential ingredient for positive relationships. He has captured the essence of trust and the courage it takes to be a high-trust leader committed to developing cohesive, effective, and highly productive teams."
—**Howard A. "Art" Dillon, Jr.,** Brigadier General, US Army (Ret)

"*Trustology* is breakthrough thinking on a topic we all think we know about, but don't. This book will transform the way you interact with people and lead within your organization (and in your life)."
—**Tracy Gohari,** director of Global Learning and Development, Woodward, Inc.

"I've known and worked with Richard for over fourteen years. He has a unique ability to get a big-picture point across to a broad spectrum of people in a simple, clear manner. That ability comes through in Richard's book, where he gathers his wealth of experience and years of leading, training, and working with others. After all of Richard's experience working with executive teams and employees around the world, if he sees trust as the most common denominator of successful teams, then I know I need to give it the attention it deserves in my organization."

—**David Cron,** president and CEO, Skyland Grain

"I have worked with Richard over the past twelve years and have partnered with Peak Solutions in my last two jobs. Now he's written the book that shows how to look at trust in a straightforward, practical way. This book shows his heart, character, and commitment to leading leaders. Having implemented these principles, I can attest to the fact that they work. This is bound to be a game-changer for leaders everywhere."

—**Mitch Menlove,** VP of Organizational Development and Talent, Hoerbiger

"What a fun book. Low trust has destroyed companies, damaged relationships, blown up productivity, and kept many organizations from reaching their goals. *Trustology* is a great guide to the proper thinking required to establish trust in your life and in your organization. Be prepared to think differently and look at trust in new ways. This is a quick read that is hard hitting with no fluff."

—**Larry Linne,** president and CEO, Sitkins International,
and author of *Make the Noise Go Away.*

"This book is thought-provoking, insightful, and rich with practical ideas. We have used these principles within our organization, and they work!"

—**Dan Slinger,** CEO, Stratton Equity Cooperative

"In today's human capital training world, trust is a hot topic. A plethora of workshops, books, and articles speak to it, but none so clearly and logically as this book. In *Trustology*, Richard provides an effective field guide to the subject and a clear, logical path to developing trust, perfect as a tool for business teams or as a personal read. When I was a child, my mother told me, 'If you want friends, first be a friend.' *Trustology* provides us with a similar proverb: If you want trust, give trust."

—**Russ Weathers,** CEO, Agriculture Future of America

TRUST•OL•O•GY

TRUST•OL•O•GY

THE ART AND SCIENCE OF
LEADING HIGH-TRUST TEAMS

RICHARD FAGERLIN

WISEGUYS
PRESS

Trustology
Published by Wise Guys Press
1112 Oakridge Drive, Suite 104-277
Fort Collins, CO 80525

Cover design by Kristopher Orr
Interior design and illustrations by Toolbox Creative
Edited by Laura Tucker

Library of Congress Cataloging-in-Publication Data

Fagerlin, Richard.
Trustology : the art and science of leading high-trust teams /
by Richard Fagerlin.
ISBN: 978-0-9893916-0-3 (paperback) – ISBN: 978-0-9893916-1-0 (electronic)
1. Business & economics / leadership 2. Business & economics / mentoring & coaching 3. Family & relationships / interpersonal relations

2011006922

Printed in the United States of America.
2013–First Edition
10 9 8 7 6 5 4 3 2 1

Special Sales
For special quantity discounts for your corporation, organization, or special-interest group, please contact Wise Guys Press at www.wiseguyspress.com.

To my best friend and wife, Christy,
I love our life together.

To my courageous warriors,
Christian, Preston, Jackson, and Lincoln,
I love being your dad.

The best way to find out if you can trust somebody is to trust them.

—Ernest Hemingway

TABLE OF CONTENTS

Trustology 301: Leading High-Trust Teams

FOREWORD

What one thing most determines the success of teams, businesses, leaders, and personal relationships?

The answer is trust.

From the years I've spent working with and developing leaders around the world, I can testify that many of the problems facing organizations today can be traced back to a lack of trust. It disrupts and destroys personal relationships, teams, and entire companies. Trust is one of the most relevant issues in business and in life, and unfortunately one of the least considered and understood.

We don't need research studies to show us the costs of low trust, because we witness them every day. But consider the benefits of high trust, which opens up a world of possibilities: we accomplish more, love what we do, and enjoy the people we do it with.

How do we create high levels of trust?

Enter *Trustology*. This book is full of stick-with-you principles to help you take ownership of trust. It confronts our culture's entitlement mentality, shows why trust is worth the risk, and outlines exactly how to build trust with others. Finally, it leaves readers with a simple process to develop a high-trust culture in their teams.

Richard's message is timely and needed. His style is straightforward and he has a gift for making complicated subjects simple and leaving readers with tools they can immediately put to work. He concisely communicates many of the principles I most deeply believe in, such as servant leadership, personal responsibility, and intentionality. Any leader, team member, or individual who wants strong, successful relationships needs to read this book.

I believe that everyone has the opportunity to lead, every day. Anyone at any level can influence the world around them. The same goes for trust. It doesn't matter what your position is, how long you've been at your job, or whether you run a family business, a PTA committee, or a billion-dollar company. You can choose to lead trust. It's not about a to-do list; it's about a mindset—one of great courage, commitment, and initiative. If you are willing to change your mindset, you are ready for *Trustology*. You will learn to be a high-trust leader and show others how to do the same.

Mark Sanborn
Founder, Sanborn & Associates, Inc.
Bestselling author of *The Fred Factor* and *You Don't Need a Title to Be a Leader*

Note from the Author

I don't know what brings you to this book. Maybe you want to see your team achieve greater synergy and cooperation. Maybe your organization has experienced a lot of change, and you want to reestablish high levels of trust between your executives, managers, and employees. Maybe you have a relationship where low trust causes misunderstandings, hurt, and drained energy. Maybe your boss made you read it.

Whatever your starting place, building high-trust relationships is doable and worth it. It won't be easy, but I want to help make it simple.

This book is not a 350-page academic textbook full of studies and statistics. You wouldn't read half of it, you'd remember even less, and you'd probably have little idea how to apply it in your daily life. Instead, it's a field guide for the trenches of trust, the day-in, day-out challenges of building trust between flawed human beings. It's not for the faint of heart, not for those who want to point their fingers and shift responsibility to the other guy. It's for the leader who is tired of the status quo and willing to try something new for the sake of a future that's worth having.

I've worked with hundreds of businesses and thousands of individuals on this topic, and the principles I am about to share are not just big ideas and empty philosophy. These are tested and proven techniques that have helped change the face of businesses and reclaim relationships.

My hope is that this book is more than a temporary dose of motivation or entertainment. I hope that it offers you a new mindset on a common topic, a fresh vision for the future, and greatly enriched relationships, both personal and professional.

Richard Fagerlin
President, Peak Solutions

TRUSTOLOGY:
AN INTRODUCTION

Of the thousands of books published each year on leadership, management, self-help, and motivation, very few offer practical tools and solutions to the number one challenge in business (and in most of our personal lives): trust.

With trust, our relationships flourish, our productivity rises, and we have high personal and professional satisfaction. A trust-filled atmosphere lets people take risks, allowing innovation and creativity to thrive. Your team's collective sense of self-worth and purpose becomes a beacon of light for others to follow. The healthy, dynamic atmosphere is contagious, and it raises the bar for your entire organization. Higher productivity and lower turnover creates a more profitable business. High trust is the currency of greatness.

High-performance teams are tight-knit groups of skilled individuals closely focused on a common goal and willing to overcome all obstacles to achieve it. They out-perform their peers in quality, speed, and a positive working atmosphere. This type of team cannot exist without trust.

Without trust, on the other hand, we protect our own interests, productivity plummets, and our personal satisfaction and professional engagement hit all-time lows. Low trust is the highest predictor of re-work—wasted time spent redoing a task. When trust is lacking, we spend so much time and energy covering our bases, protecting our turf, and creating alliances that we can't do anything effectively.

Over the last twelve years I have worked with business and community leaders all around the world. Some have formal titles, while others simply lead from the pack. But no matter what type of organization they're from, all our clients want the same thing from our firm: help creating a powerful vision and strategy for the future, and making that vision a reality. The solutions are diverse, but the problems we see along the way are painfully similar. Almost all of them are rooted in an issue of trust.

> **Trust isn't what we "do"—it's what results from what we do.**

Our firm doesn't specialize in "trust building." We are not fans of climbing on rocks and ropes to mysteriously become a great team and have high trust. We won't ask our clients to climb on a table and fall into each other's hands. Trust isn't what we "do"—it's what results from what we do.

Trust is the single most important factor in determining whether a group of individuals will become a high-functioning, high-performance team. With all of that at stake, it's time to be intentional about trust.

In this book, we're going to address questions like:

- What is trust?

- Is trust earned?

- Who is responsible for trust?

- How do you grow trust with others?

- What does it mean to be trustworthy?

- How can I lead my team to be a high-trust team?

- How do I find out how much trust my team has now?

- How can team members hold each other accountable for high-trust behavior?

Any high-trust relationship involves at least two people, so there are always two things to think about regarding trust: Do you trust them? Do they trust you? The premise of this book is that both are your responsibility.

In Trustology 101, we'll look at the first part of that equation, your choice to trust. We'll examine a popular myth about trust and where it falls short, compare the risks and rewards of trust, and talk about practical ways to show that you trust someone.

In Trustology 202, we'll move on to how you show yourself trustworthy so that you can increase your Trust Factor with others.

> A high-trust relationship requires that you trust the other person and that they trust you back. The premise of this book is that both are your responsibility.

And in Trustology 303, we'll look at how you can develop a high-trust team.

Ready for Trustology 101?

TRUSTOLOGY 101:

TRUST
STARTS HERE

TRUST'S BIG LIE

As we embark on our informal study of trust, it's worth noting that no one comes to this discussion empty-handed. We all have strong feelings about trust. We know how it feels when it is misused, betrayed, or withheld. Our perspectives have been informed by a lifetime of valid personal experiences, but sometimes the conclusions we've drawn from those experiences don't help us. In fact, they can hold us hostage.

Over the years that I've spent helping teams work through interpersonal trust dynamics, I've come to a surprising conclusion: our most popular theories about trust are often untrue and almost always unhelpful.

Before we go any further, I should warn you. Some of the things I'm about to say might go against everything you've ever heard about trust. Whenever I speak to a group on this topic, I start by asking them to set aside their preconceptions and objections for a few minutes so they can join me as we look at trust from a fresh perspective. Would you do the same? Would you be willing to put aside your experiences and beliefs about trust for a little while? If you still think I'm crazy by the end of this book, you are most certainly entitled to continue believing as you choose. But if you, like me, begin to feel the inadequacy of the old theories, we can leave them behind and find a better way.

Of all the flawed theories flying around about trust, there is one that is more prevalent, more seemingly intuitive, and more damaging than any other:

Trust's Big Lie: Trust is something that is *earned.*

The Truth on Trust: Trust can't be earned. It can only be *given.*

When we're deciding how much to trust people, we usually ask ourselves whether they have earned our trust. That seems like the smart thing to do. Until they earn it, we withhold trust to protect ourselves. We put defensive policies in place. We micromanage to maintain control.

But the truth is, trust can never be earned. Trust can only be given.

Trust is the responsibility of the person who wants high trust. Presumably, you. If you are committed to giving and building trust, and determined to overcome any obstacles that stand in your way, you will win high trust. If you work patiently and with perseverance to lead your team towards a high-trust, high-performance culture, you can see it happen.

The ten most powerful two-letter words in the English language are *if it is to be, it is up to me.*

If you are to have high trust in your relationships, it starts and ends with you.

> **If you are to have high trust in your relationships, it starts and ends with you.**

SURRENDER THE SCORECARD

So why doesn't it work for trust to be earned? Surely that's the safer route, right? If trust could be earned, someone would have to be keeping score. I imagine that everyone who operates out of this belief has a huge internal scorecard for all their relationships. If someone does something trustworthy, they get two ticker marks. But if they do something untrustworthy, they are at risk of losing the last two ticker marks and perhaps three or four more.

According to British anthropologist Robin Dunbar, the number of human beings with whom a person can maintain stable social relationships is remarkably consistent from person to person. The Dunbar number, as it is called, is proposed to be somewhere between 100 and 230, with 150 as the commonly used average. In other words, the average person has about 150 social relationships, not necessarily including casual acquaintances, former friends, or distant connections on social media.

With so many legitimate human interactions to manage, how on earth can we accurately keep track of how much trust each person has earned? That kind of scorekeeping is bound to be inaccurate, and it's definitely complicated and confusing. Do you like the feeling of being constantly evaluated? Neither does anyone else.

In a business context, keeping score is even less practical. A business's success depends on productivity, efficiency, and high morale, and scorekeeping drains those things dry. If companies had to start out every new client or employee at zero trust until they proved themselves, it would cripple the team's ability to operate efficiently or to take risks. The more high-performing the team, the more it requires the safety of unconditional trust.

Wikipedia describes the high-performance team as a group of people with complementary talents, roles, and skills, aligned with and committed to a common purpose, who consistently show high levels of collaboration and innovation and produce superior results. Or, as I like to define it, a group where every individual is a contributing partner to the success of the team. Team members are tight-knit and focused, so devoted to their purpose that they will surmount any barrier to achieve the team's goals.

> The more high-performance a team, the more it requires the safety of unconditional trust.

Now imagine that kind of a team withholding trust, guarding their own backs, and keeping track of each other's failures and successes. It wouldn't work for a second. Teams who want high efficiency and morale must be proactive about giving trust.

Trust cannot be earned; it can only be given. When we insist on keeping score, everyone loses.

QUIT YOUR JOB:
YOU ARE NOT THE TRUST REF

Since it's impossible to keep score, it's time to submit your resignation letter as the referee of your relationships. Time to stop keeping tabs of who is ahead in thoughtful, trust-earning behavior. If you are like me, this won't be easy. I trust ref my friends, I trust ref my colleagues, and I even trust ref my wife.

As we study trust in the context of organizational teams, we can learn a lot by taking a minute to think about how trust works in other relationships, such as in a marriage. Now, I'm not saying we have the same kind of trust with colleagues as we do with our spouses, but similar principles are at work across the board.

> **I trust ref my friends, my colleagues, and even my wife.**

I love my wife very much. We have been married for more than fifteen years, have four wonderful children together, and are truly best friends. But I still struggle with quitting my job as the trust ref on a daily basis.

I want nothing more than to see my wife thrive. To see her vibrant and doing what she loves. I want her to be encouraged and loved in a deep way—and then I become a bonehead. I find myself counting up my good deeds and her not-so-good deeds. I hope that you can't identify with this, but, chances are, you can identify a great deal. Giving trust without keeping a record of rights and wrongs isn't easy, but it is essential to win the war for relationships.

Marriages start out with weddings: blissful days where every detail has been thoughtfully arranged and everyone is on their best behavior. The couple vows their love and undying commitment. But then what happens? Half of today's marriages end, with tremendous costs to society. Many who have experienced divorce can give good reasons for it, but few would say they went into the relationship expecting it to fail. So how did they get there? What led from the hopefulness of the wedding day to such a deep level of relational dysfunction? I suggest that it is usually a breakdown in trust.

At the wedding of my good friend's son, the pastor said something to the bride and groom that has stuck with me ever since. He said, "Your goal is to take second place. You are to see that the other gets first place. You are to sacrifice for them, love them, and make sure that you don't keep a record of right or wrong."

That phrase comes from a common reading at wedding ceremonies, a Bible passage from 1 Corinthians 13:

"Love is patient, love is kind. It does not envy, it does
not boast, it is not proud. It does not dishonor others,
it is not self-seeking, it is not easily angered, it keeps

no record of wrongs. Love does not delight in evil but rejoices with the truth. It always protects, always trusts, always hopes, always perseveres."

What if the word *love* was replaced by *trust?*

Trust is patient, trust is kind. Trust does not envy, trust does not boast, trust is not proud. Trust does not dishonor others, trust is not self-seeking, trust is not easily angered, trust keeps no record of wrongs. Trust does not delight in evil but rejoices with the truth. Trust always protects, always trusts, always hopes, always perseveres.

Trust keeps no record of wrongs. Once you've made a decision to trust someone, once you've decided that winning at that relationship is non-negotiable, you have to stop keeping score—and this is true whether the relationship is with a spouse or a colleague.

Stop keeping track of their good and bad deeds, of whether they've had as many good ideas as you or worked through as many lunches.

Not keeping a record of wrongs doesn't mean ignoring a bad situation. Address genuine problems head-on—but don't make trust conditional upon a person's good score. Trust them. If conflict does need to happen, it will go much better when it happens from a place of trust.

Don't make trust conditional upon a person's good score.

NOT SAFE, BUT GOOD

The number one reason why trust cannot be earned is that even if we could find a perfect way to keep score of the performance of every one of our team members, no one could do enough good things to guarantee that they wouldn't disappoint us in the future.

Trust has never existed in a risk-free environment. No matter how well you know someone, given enough opportunities, everyone will fall short in some way or another. High-trust teams are strong, but it's a strength that comes through mutual vulnerability. If you are not willing to accept the fundamental vulnerability of high-trust teams, you'll never have one. At some point, each of the parties involved will have to take the risk of giving trust.

In C. S. Lewis's children's book *The Lion, The Witch, and the Wardrobe*, the Pevensie children are quite nervous when they find out that Aslan, the king of Narnia, is not a man but a lion. Susan, the eldest, asks,

"Is he—quite safe? I shall feel rather nervous about meeting a lion."

"That you will, dearie, and no mistake," said Mrs. Beaver; "if there's anyone who can appear before Aslan without their knees knocking, they're either braver than most or else just silly."

"Then he isn't safe?" said Lucy.

"Safe?" said Mr. Beaver; "don't you hear what Mrs. Beaver tells you? Who said anything about safe? 'Course he isn't safe. But he's good."

> **If you are not willing to accept the fundamental vulnerability of high-trust teams, you'll never have one.**

Giving trust is not safe. But it's good. It's always a risk, but it's always worth it.

PLAY THE ODDS

Even though trust is not "safe," it can still be a wise invest-ment. The question is, do the rewards outweigh the risks?

Everyone will eventually disappoint you in small ways. (And guess what? You'll disappoint them, too.) A few people may betray you outright. But consider for a moment how many people we're really talking about. How many people, of all those in your life, are really going to take advantage of you if you offer trust before it is earned? Twenty percent? Ten? Two?

I guess that, on average, the number is closer to two percent than it is to twenty. Yes, a few people may abuse your trust. But do you want to live and act for the two percent or the ninety-eight percent?

> Do you want to live and act for the two percent or the ninety-eight percent?

Imagine a weights and measures scale. Put the risk of the two percent on one side, and the benefit of a trusting, generous relationship with the ninety-eight percent on the other. Which is heavier?

In a business, would you gain more profit by fortifying yourself against the outlier, or by being generous with the vast majority of your customers?

I contend that you win a great deal more by giving trust than you would benefit from never being burned.

98%

2%

A DISCLAIMER

I know many of you are sitting there thinking of all the situations where giving unearned trust doesn't make sense. Keep two things in mind:

First, I'm assuming the relationships in question are ones where you actually want to win, where you have a vested interest in the relationship being the best it can be, and where collaboration is critical. If that's the case, let's apply these ideas. If not, you don't need to invest time or energy into building trust.

Second, I am not speaking to the extremes. If you have experienced a betrayal of trust amounting to psychological or physical abuse, address it appropriately. Ask a friend for help, get a counselor, talk to a mentor, or read one of the many great books out there that address healing and boundaries on a personal level. This book is not a one-stop-shop for rebuilding shattered trust.

Most of life should not be a crisis.

But most of life should not be a crisis. I want to speak to the rest of the time, to normal person-to-person interactions. I want to address the boss who wants a strong team. The employee who wants to be trusted with more opportunities. The person who wants to increase trust in a relationship. If that's you, welcome. Let's explore these ideas together.

EYES WIDE OPEN

Trust must be given, not earned, but I'm not advocating blind trust.

My wife and I have four boys: Christian, Preston, Jackson, and Lincoln. When they were little, the street in front of our house was completely off-limits. The risk was too great. But if they were still afraid to cross the street as thirteen-year-olds, or twenty-year-olds, we'd have a problem. I want my boys to wisely take risks that are worth taking, and not to live in fear. But I don't want them to walk across the street with their eyes closed. I want them to have their eyes wide open and look both ways. And then to walk forward.

In the same way, I'm not asking you to plunge ahead foolishly, but to make a mature, calculated, thoughtful decision to trust because you've decided the benefits outweigh the risks.

By all means, be aware of red flags when you sense that someone isn't trustworthy. Red flags don't necessarily mean that there's no way forward, but you should ask where they are coming from, be more careful in the steps that you take, and set appropriate boundaries. You should make difficult judgment calls when your role requires it, and not turn a blind eye to systemic issues. But even if you've experienced a breakdown in trust in the past, don't let that take away your choice to trust as you move forward.

Not blind trust. Eyes-wide-open trust.

RELEASE YOUR HOSTAGES

The idea that trust is given, not earned, is a big mind-shift for most of us. It requires that we quit keeping score and become willing to give trust even when we don't receive anything in return. This may feel a bit uncomfortable. The truth is, this shift brings freedom. Freedom from carrying around another person's failures. Freedom to give yourself and the other person a fresh start. Freedom to allow yourself to forgive and let go.

The old score-keeping mindset, where we are counting up our team members' trustworthy behavior so we can add more ticker marks to our scorecard, holds them and us hostage.

"Really, Richard?" you might say. "Isn't 'hostage' a little extreme?" I don't think so. You may not be throwing your colleagues into a dungeon full of rats, but they certainly aren't living their best, at least not in their relationship with you.

When we choose to be judge and jury in our relationships, we don't publicize our rules and guidelines. We judge the other person's words, actions, and intentions by our own past experiences. How do we expect the other person to win our game when they don't even know the rules?

One of the most important ways that we can give unearned trust is to assume the best about people's intentions and give them a chance to explain their perspective. When we don't, we hold them hostage to our assumptions.

> **When you punish others by making them feel your hurt until they feel sufficiently guilty, you hold them hostage.**

When you stand back evaluating the other person's every move and marking pluses and minuses on your scorecard, you hold them hostage to your eternal evaluation. When you punish them by making them feel your hurt until you think they feel sufficiently guilty, you hold them hostage to your pain.

My dad once said, "Peace and unity are at risk when questions and debate are limited." Next time you find yourself so angry that you stop caring to hear the other person's point of view, ask yourself if you are holding them hostage to your own resentment. If you are, stop, apologize, and ask the other person to share their perspective. Say something like, "This is how what you did made me feel, although I don't believe you meant to hurt me. Can you tell me where you're coming from?"

Simply offering people the chance to speak for themselves gives them the benefit of the doubt and is one step forward in giving trust.

QUIT DRINKING POISON

Does the idea of releasing people from the ways they have disappointed you, or giving trust to someone who hasn't earned it, seem like condoning bad behavior? Sometimes we hold people hostage as a way of protesting their irresponsible or unfair actions. We think we're teaching them a lesson, but the problem is that we're holding ourselves hostage as well. When we withhold forgiveness, we keep ourselves stuck in a place of mistrust and suspicion.

A very wise person once said, "Resentment is like drinking poison and waiting for the other person to die." Unforgiveness harms us far more than it hurts the other person, and usually far more than the original offense itself. It colors how we see people. It keeps us from assuming the best about others, even those who had nothing to do with the initial violation. It infects us like a virus, eating up innocence and leaving cynicism and bitterness behind. It's not the original offense that makes anyone bitter. It's when we hold on to it, plant it deep in our hearts, and water it with every fresh offense.

If we hold on to unforgiveness, we won't be able to have high trust with the person who wronged us or with anyone else.

Resentment is like drinking poison and waiting for the other person to die.

Forgiveness is not about excusing bad behavior. Forgiveness is simply about letting yourself move on. Forgiveness is saying to the other person, "You don't owe me." It doesn't mean that what they did was okay, but it does mean that you surrender your right to be their judge and jury. You relinquish your right to be their debt collector.

If we want to have high trust in our relationships and within our teams, we need to embrace the idea that we are not our own avengers. Life is not about achieving fairness for ourselves. If life isn't about fairness, then it has to be about freedom. And if it's about freedom, then we have to forgive. And when we do, we release ourselves, too. From that moment, we are no longer stuck.

Is there anyone you need to forgive to set yourself free? Is there an old offense that creeps into every new disagreement, or someone you blame, even in a small way, for the way your life or career has turned out? Is there anyone with whom past frustrations have reduced down to a murky, indefinable bad taste in your mouth whenever you have to work with them?

Becoming willing to forgive can be hard, but the actual moment of forgiveness is incredibly easy. It's as easy as letting a heavy backpack you've been carrying drop to the floor. You might realize ten minutes later you've picked the backpack back up and have to set it down all over again. That's okay. Just keep letting it go. This isn't a sprint. It's a marathon. Just keep taking one step at a time in the direction you want to go.

Are you ready to quit drinking the poison? You will be glad you did.

WIMPS NEED NOT APPLY

Have you ever known anyone who seemed to think that forgiveness was giving in, that trust was a sign of weakness, and that putting themselves in a vulnerable position would make them needy? The truth is entirely the opposite.

The decision to trust is a profoundly free act. Only a confident, courageous person can choose to trust.

When managers decide to stop controlling their teams through stifling policies and perpetual hovering (figurative or literal), and instead find more creative ways to empower their people to excellence, they are authentically strong leaders.

The decision to trust is a profoundly free act.

When a team decides to embrace healthy conflict and honest feedback for the sake of winning a higher level of interpersonal trust, they are a courageous team.

When a person decides to forgive a wrong so that both parties can be free, they are brave.

Far from being a sign of weakness, mature vulnerability can only come from a place of strength.

HIGH TRUST
IN PRACTICE

We've talked about how high-trust relationships start with you, the person who wants high trust, giving trust to another person without knowing whether you'll get anything in return. But what does it look like to communicate, on a practical level, that you trust someone?

People will believe that you trust them when you take time to know them personally, you respect them, and you give them influence. Below are some practical ways you can show trust to individuals and create a larger team culture of trust.

Listen, Learn, and Like. It goes a long way with people when you sincerely listen to them with the intent to learn. If you want to give trust, show interest. Find out where they're coming from, especially when you disagree. This communicates that you assume they're reasonable, well-intentioned people. Find something you like about them. You don't have to become best friends, but it should be your goal to like them.

Relentlessly pursue their strengths. Figure out what they are good at and what comes easily for them, and draw it out. Bring attention to it. Give them opportunities to shine. The more they work in their strengths, the more value they add to the team and the more they value their work.

Create an Individual Development Plan (IDP) with goals and commitments from the employee and from their boss. Create a game plan for growing, learning, and adding more value.

> **People will believe that you trust them when you take time to know them, you respect them, and you give them influence.**

Share your leadership responsibilities. Give your team members assignments to lead certain aspects of your team. Let them run meetings, plan events, coordinate customer site visits, or participate in the planning and budgeting process. Let go of the reigns a bit and give them some freedom.

Get over yourself. Let's be honest. One of the main reasons you may not like relinquishing control to someone else is that you believe you are better, smarter, and more qualified than they are. Stop that. How did you get where you are? Likely by someone better, smarter, and more qualified getting out of your way.

Allow growth and expect failures. Not everyone succeeds on the first try, and nobody succeeds always. Be willing to push people to grow, and in doing so, expect failure. Celebrate it. Failure is education, and if we don't fail we won't learn. As Henry Ford said, those who never make mistakes work for those who do.

Expose them to the larger process. I intentionally introduce my four boys to people and concepts that are above their current level of understanding. They might not understand a conversation about balancing a checkbook, but they're seeing what it means to be an adult. The same holds true in business. Exposing your team members to decision makers, stakeholders, clients, macro-level discussions, and other aspects of your organization that are above their current job description communicates that you trust them, you expect them to advance, and you're invested in their future.

> Expose your team to people, discussions, and concepts above their pay grade.

Ask your team for ideas. Hold innovation bursts where you brainstorm ideas for improvements, find opportunities for efficiencies, create new ideas, and improve old ones. Collect these ideas and implement something. If you can't implement an idea, let them know, but if you can, do!

Get good at defining projects. Give your team projects with defined time frames and goals, make sure they have the resources they need, and then set them loose. Let them know what you desire as an outcome, but let them figure out how to get there. This allows you to give more freedom and them to take initiative, while minimizing frustration for all involved.

Work when and where it makes sense. Not everyone can or should work from home (or at the lake, or in the evening, or from a coffee shop). But when it makes sense, allow flexibility in how your team gets their work done. Trust them to manage their results.

Look for opportunities to say yes. Instead of saying no to your team's unusual requests, instead think, "What needs to happen so I can say yes?"

Support their passions. If you support volunteerism and corporate giving, come alongside your team members and allow them to direct where you give. Let them volunteer for a cause they care about, or provide some level of match to their existing giving.

HIGH TRUST RESULTS

For each of the last several years, my team and I have taken a different group of leaders from a certain company through a year-long development series. As part of the series, each year's group was asked to plan out a project for the company to work on. In the past, this honestly hadn't gone too well. The executive team had assigned projects and leaders, and no one had very high expectations for the results. Very few of the projects were actually implemented.

My team observed that we hadn't actually been showing great trust by providing tight controls and low expectations. As it came time to roll out the projects with this year's group, we approached it totally differently.

This year, we helped the group of leaders brainstorm different projects that would have a strategic impact on their company. The group narrowed the list down, individuals self-selected their projects, we didn't assign an executive leader, and we allowed groups to be self-paced. We provided clear expectations and required each group to submit a project outline so we could make sure everyone's efforts would be aligned. The result was an amazing six months of work and one hundred percent implementation of all projects. At the end of the program the group presented their final results to the executive team and showed several million dollars of real gain for the business during that year, as well as an assumed benefit of over $1.5 million ongoing year after year.

Those teams flourished when they were trusted with low controls and high expectations. Giving trust is good for business, good for leaders, and good for teams.

DISCOVERY QUESTIONS

Have you experienced a betrayal of trust in the past? How has that influenced your understanding of trust? How does it affect the way you interact with people?

What would you stand to gain from a higher level of trust in your relationships?

What might eyes-wide-open trust look like in your life?

What are three specific ways you can give trust this week?

TRUSTOLOGY 201:
BUILDING TRUST WITH OTHERS

THE LEADER'S CONTRADICTION

In Trustology 101 we confronted Trust's Big Lie—the belief that trust is earned—with the truth that trust must be given. High-trust relationships start with our choice to extend unearned trust to others. It may not be safe, but the rewards of high-trust teams far outweigh the risks.

But once we choose to set things in motion by offering trust to our teams, what about their decisions to trust us in return? Are we off the hook? No! We have a responsibility there also—and that's a good thing, because where there is responsibility there is opportunity. We can do something about it. We can show ourselves worthy of trust.

"Wait a minute," you might be saying. "You're talking about being worthy of trust, but doesn't that go against the idea that trust isn't earned?" If that sounds like a contradiction to you, you're not alone. Most of the questions I've gotten about trust over the years have to do with linking those two concepts together.

Remember the premise of this book. *There are two parts to a high-trust relationship. You must trust them, and they must trust you. Both are your responsibility.*

If this premise is a contradiction, it's the contradiction that every good leader knows well: As leaders, we hold ourselves to a higher standard. Leaders take the initiative to give unearned trust. And leaders accept responsibility to show themselves trustworthy.

The best way I can explain it is that in the human equation, you are only responsible for the side of the equation that you are on. You are only responsible for what you can do. When you are the truster, you are responsible to give trust, without knowing if you'll get anything back. That is the only way you will close the gap between you and the other person. When you are the trustee, the person wanting to be trusted, you are responsible to show yourself trustworthy.

> ## Where there is responsibility, there is opportunity.

You are only responsible for you. You can't control the other person's willingness to trust. You can't control whether or not they are trustworthy. But you can control yourself. You can choose to offer trust and at the same time you can choose to do things that make you a trustworthy person. *I have never seen anyone persevere in doing these two things and not win a high-trust relationship.*

I am not saying that this is easy. In fact, in case you haven't gotten this yet, this is hard, really hard. There are risks and challenges, but only by making these sacrifices will you find that there are also rewards. This takes ownership and faith.

So how do we show ourselves trustworthy? By working the Trust Model.

THE TRUST MODEL

Trust is a funny thing. We have strong opinions about it, but it's a bit intangible. It's hard to nail down a concise definition of what trust is or how it's built. When we accept that it is our responsibility to show ourselves trustworthy to others, the next question is, how? What communicates trustworthiness?

Here is my definition of trust:

trust: confidence in others

Specifically, trust is confidence that

1. What a person says they will do, they will actually do. (Integrity)

2. A person has the knowledge, skills, or abilities needed to perform their job. (Competence)

3. A person has your best interests at heart. (Compassion)

Confidence equals predictability, and predictability, when it comes to high-trust relationships, is king.

Together, confidence in integrity, confidence in competence, and confidence in compassion make a three-legged stool of trust. When you have all three, trust will be strong.

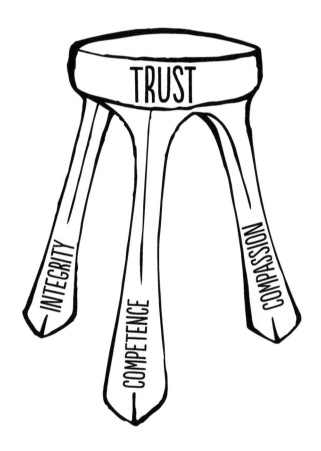

The Trust Model serves two functions:

First, it can help you diagnose why you find it difficult to trust someone. Once you know which leg of the stool is weak, you will be better able to address the situation and get to a place where you can give trust. We'll discuss this more in the chapter called "Breaking the Stalemate."

Second, working the Trust Model is the way that you develop trust with others by showing yourself trustworthy.

Let's look more closely at each leg of the stool in turn.

INTEGRITY

The first leg of the stool is confidence in integrity: who a person is.

in•teg•ri•ty: consistent adherence to moral and ethical principles; the quality of being complete or undivided

For someone to trust you, they must have confidence that you are an honest, dependable person who will do what you say you will do.

The root of the word *integrity* is *integer*. An integer in mathematics is a whole number. A person with integrity is a whole person. They are consistent. They are the same whether you see them at work on a Tuesday afternoon, at home on a Friday evening, or in church on a Sunday morning.

When a client, supervisor, or coworker has integrity, it creates a working environment characterized by safety and loyalty. People assume the best about that person, and they aren't disappointed.

OVER-DELIVER ON YOUR PROMISES

I once had a boss who was not only an extremely competent and driven individual, but also a man of high character and integrity. I started working for him with the promise of a significant salary increase and relocation to a new job in the near future. Well, the new job took longer than expected to materialize. In the meantime, I had all the responsibilities of the new position without the formal title and salary adjustment. Although I was frustrated that I didn't get the commitment in writing, I knew I had no option but to trust the process. So I waited.

Six months later, the promotion finally came through. I moved to Colorado to start my new job, and my salary adjustment was made active. One day I received a check in the mail from my boss. The check was for all of the back salary that I had earned over those six months. My boss explained that he was a man of his word, and that while it had taken time for the position to be approved, he wanted to make things right with me. This was a simple effort by him, but one that made a big impact on me. We maintain a great relationship to this day, not because he paid me well, but because his character is worthy of imitation.

THE IMPACT OF INTEGRITY

I get the opportunity to work with many people of strong character and integrity, but one in particular stands out. Greg is the president and CEO of a fourth-generation family business. I've worked with Greg and his leadership team for years, and I've seen something that is unique and inspiring. Greg cares personally for each of his employees in a way that goes beyond the norm. The loyalty and commitment from his team are unparalleled. Over the years, many of his team members have told me stories, often with tears, of how Greg has impacted their lives.

One of Greg's leaders once stood up during a strategy session to share the impact that Greg had made in his life. He said, "Greg has invested in me both personally and professionally. His confidence in me and his care for my family have changed my life." Another leader said, "Greg has never given up on me. He not only expects good things from me at work, he also expects good things from me in my personal life. With his encouragement, I'm motivated to live better. I have started working out again, going to church again, and believing in myself again after being discouraged for many years."

Greg's consistently demonstrated integrity has fostered a deep, mutual trust in his team, and he would tell you that this is a key factor in his business's success.

DISCOVERY QUESTIONS

Whom do you know who is a beacon of integrity? How does that affect your trust in them?

When your integrity is tested, what is the internal compass that helps you determine your "true north" so you can make the right decisions?

What areas of your personal and professional life do you feel are at odds with one another? If integrity is about being whole, complete, and undivided, where do you struggle making that happen?

COMPETENCE

A second leg of the stool is confidence in competence: what a person can do.

> com•pe•tence: possession of the knowledge, skills, or abilities required to get something done

In order to trust you, a person must have confidence that you will be able to accomplish what's been asked of you.

Think of someone you know who is extremely competent at what they do. They are calm and decisive under pressure. The unexpected doesn't stress them out because they know where to go to find a solution. They make what they do look easy. That kind of person is a pleasure to trust, because you know they will be able to handle whatever is thrown at them.

If you want to be trusted, be a person of competence.

Become a Knowledge Broker

Competent people constantly strive to grow in their craft, whether that's building a table, managing a team, or growing a business. They are lifelong learners. And these days, they are also knowledge brokers.

Competence used to be simply about knowledge. We lived in a knowledge era. Knowledge was power, and the more you had, the more powerful you were. All schooling, education, and training were designed to increase your know-how in a specific subject, with the goal of making you the top expert in your field.

Today, however, we live in a knowledge brokering and acquisition era. It is now more important for competence that you know where to go to acquire new knowledge and are skilled in sharing that knowledge with those around you.

Pass It On

Good knowledge brokers know how to pass on the institutional knowledge in their organizations. They pair up people with years of experience and specific technical knowledge with those who need it. They provide opportunities for people to mentor and pass along knowledge, both formally and informally.

Knowledge brokering isn't just about more experienced people passing on information to the new guys. It's about understanding who has the skills and knowledge in each area and how those people can become teachers and facilitators instead of merely subject-matter experts.

Mix It Up

The organizational development industry has seen a major shift happen over the last few years. Training sessions used to be conducted in homogenous groups, with executives, middle managers, and frontline employees all separated from one another. Instead, we're now seeing people from different levels brought together in cross-functional groups, with dynamic results. This makes sense—since these groups of leaders are solving problems and running their businesses together, why shouldn't they learn to learn together?

As you build a culture of knowledge brokering in your organization, remember to look for ways to bring people together across levels and departments. Not only will this make your team aware of the wealth of knowledge residing in their fellow employees, but it will also help each person feel appreciated and connected to the larger goals of the company. (Bonus: It will also increase the third element of trust, compassion.)

KNOW WHERE TO LOOK

A key strength of the knowledge broker is knowing how to best acquire new, accurate knowledge quickly.

I am currently preparing a keynote address on how HR professionals can rework their touchy-feely image and be seen as serious business partners to their executive teams. I asked people in my network, including connections on the professional networking site LinkedIn, to contribute their best practices and ideas for my presentation. Isn't it fantastic that I can get the input of a few hundred professionals for my 60-minute talk? I don't have to have all of the answers myself, and my audience gets to benefit from the cumulative wisdom of these on-the-ground experts. My ability to broker other people's knowledge increases my competence, builds trust, and increases the competence of my listeners, all at the same time.

Where do you and your team go to find just-in-time information or solutions? If "Google it" is all that comes to mind, also
consider:

- Knowledge forums within your field
- Industry blogs
- Websites
- Informal surveys of your customers through a social media post
- Think tanks with cross-functional groups of colleagues

Consider asking each of your team members to contribute
their most frequently referenced sources for an internal go-to
resource list.

There are also many things that you can do on a larger scale,
before the crunch, to develop a culture of knowledge brokering in
your organization:

- Industry meetings, live streams, and conferences
- A series of lunchtime presentations from each department about how they serve the overall mission of your company
- Mentoring relationships
- Continuing education, certification courses, and seminars
- Volunteer and community service opportunities

Good knowledge brokers have what it takes to succeed in
today's ever-changing workplace. As other people see that you are
not only skilled in your subject area but also know where to go to
get new information as the need arises, their confidence in your
competence rises, and their trust in you grows.

DISCOVERY QUESTIONS

Are you the resident genius in any particular area? If so, what are you doing to help broker your knowledge to others in your organization?

How can you provide opportunities for your team members to grow from each other's knowledge and strengths?

What are your team's top sources for quick knowledge? Are there any potential sources you have overlooked?

When people don't have the competence required to gain the respect and trust of others, what can you do to help them?

COMPASSION

The third leg of the stool, and probably the most elusive, is confidence in compassion: how a person relates.

> **com•pas•sion: empathy for and understanding of others**

In order to trust you, a person must have confidence that you care about them and that you seek to understand their position.

Compassion isn't a fluffy, lovey, kumbaya feeling. Compassion is real, tough, and one of the most important components in building trust.

Simply defined, compassion is having empathy for and understanding of others. In his book *The Seven Habits of Highly Effective People*, Stephen Covey explains compassion as a habit of seeking first to understand before being understood.

Compassionate people are guided by the belief that people are doing their best. They assume the best about others' motives and intentions. They can easily envision themselves in another person's situation and have a high degree of care and concern for the people around them.

Tough Compassion

Compassion doesn't always mean everyone is getting along. Not long ago I worked with a client whose marketing director was an absolute cancer to the group. Her work wasn't stellar, but, more importantly, she wasn't a good team member. She was rude and condescending and constantly questioned other people's motives. The people that worked for her feared her, and the other managers created workarounds so that they wouldn't have to utilize the services of her team.

It was obvious that she needed to go. Obvious to everyone but her boss, the CEO. He knew that she was a problem to the team, and he even agreed that her work was substandard. But he thought that he needed to continue to give her the chance to improve, and he took it as a personal challenge to make her better.

In one meeting I said to him, "You seem to have quite the culture of grace around here." He said thank you. I smiled and said, "I'm not sure I meant that as a compliment."

I'm not saying grace isn't important; it's critical, but so is discernment. While the CEO was being gracious to this one manager, he was, as a result, being totally ungracious to everyone she worked with. He was losing compassion, competence, and perhaps integrity in the eyes of all his employees the longer he allowed her negative behavior. I helped him see that the most gracious thing he could do was to let this woman go, releasing her from an environment that was making everyone, including her, miserable.

Later that day he fired her. His grace took the form of a generous severance package. We learned later that she went on to another company and position that are better fits for her. She is satisfied, her self-worth is high, and she is no longer miserable. And neither are her former colleagues.

Compassion can come in a lot of packages, and sometimes it happens to come in difficult decisions and cold, hard truth.

DISCOVERY QUESTIONS

Would others consider you to be a compassionate person? Do you have a concern for and understanding of others that shows you really care?

How could you better communicate your compassion?

Are you being overly gracious in any particular area? Do you need to extend tough love?

TRUST FACTOR

We've looked at three components of trust: confidence in integrity, confidence in competence, and confidence in compassion. Together they create the Trust Model's three-legged stool. Every time there is a lack of trust, whether in a team, an organization, or a personal relationship, it's because of a lack of confidence in one of these three areas.

The degree to which the other person has confidence in all three of these characteristics is your Trust Factor.

trust fac•tor: the degree to which someone has confidence in another person's integrity, competence, and compassion; the place where trust flourishes

Picture a Venn diagram on the top of our trust stool, with one circle for each leg. The central area where all three circles overlap is your Trust Factor. The bigger it is, the more a person will trust you. The smaller it is, the more difficult it will be to establish trust.

To grow the Trust Factor of a relationship, simply demonstrate your integrity, competence, and compassion. This is "working the Trust Model."

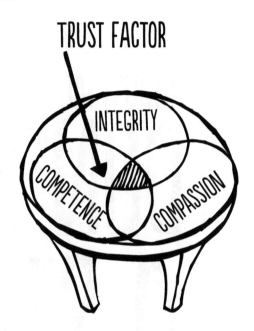

A TRUST FACTOR CASE STUDY:
DON'T BE A STAN

Years ago, when I took my first 360-degree feedback assessment, I was rudely awakened to a new reality: I wasn't the manager I thought I was.

Thankfully, I had a consultant there to help me understand my assessment results and put them into context. According to the assessment, my team felt stifled because I always had to have the last word. The funny thing was, I had consistently heard this feedback before, but always in the context of my personal life. I thought I was doing things better at work.

In an effort to learn more, I first met with my team and thanked them for the feedback. (After all, that was the mature thing to do, right?) I explained the consistent theme from my assessment and told my team that I wanted to grow in this area. Then I told them that during our next one-on-one meetings I wanted each of them to share how this fault of mine was affecting them and how I could improve.

After meeting with everyone over the next week or two, I came to the conclusion that I had become the guy who always had to say something. The guy who had to add something to someone's idea, who never just let it be. One of my team members referred to this as a STAN. (Shoot, that ain't nothing!)

I didn't want to be a STAN. I hate STANs. The trouble was, I didn't see myself that way. I didn't intend to have the last word. I didn't intend to squash creativity and make people think I had all the answers. I just wanted to be able to throw in my ideas.

You see, not long before, I had been a member of this team. Back then, it was my job to come up with ideas during brainstorming sessions, just like the rest of my colleagues. After I was made their supervisor, I still had creative solutions to contribute, but now it was causing problems. Why? I came to realize that my role had changed. Putting forward my own thoughts had to take a backseat to encouraging and leading my team.

I resolved to make a few changes. Instead of adding my two cents all the time, if I had more ideas, or thought the discussion could benefit from more brainstorming, I started asking questions instead of telling. Questions like:

- Do you have more ideas?

- Are there other ways we can accomplish this?

- Have we thought of other solutions?

- What alternatives do we have?

- Can you think of anything else that can make this idea stronger?

This led to better discussions, and, I am proud to say, even better ideas than the ones I had.

I resolved to say yes as much as I could, a lot more than I said no. Saying yes builds buy-in and ownership. When people stepped out, I gave them recognition. Whether it was individually or as a team, I sought ways to let them know I appreciated their work and encouraged them to step out. As I did these few things consistently, something amazing happened.

First, my compassion circle started to grow as my team felt like they were heard and understood. Then they saw me brokering their talent and ideas, and my competence circle grew as well. Over time, as they saw me make good on my promise to change, my integrity circle was affected too.

Through that one effort, all three areas of the Trust Model grew, and the trust we shared increased exponentially. I didn't need to focus on each area separately. I just focused in on a couple of things that I could do to impact the team, and all three areas were impacted.

MESSAGE SENT
VS.
MESSAGE RECEIVED

When we talk about demonstrating integrity, competence, and compassion, what we're really addressing is communication. An inconvenient but basic fact of communication is that "message sent" does not always equal "message received."

We don't lack for opportunities to communicate. We can mail, email, text, IM, blog, Instagram, Facebook, or Tweet. We get information from TV, radio, magazines, books, eBooks, newsletters, newspapers, and websites. But most of that isn't actually communication—it's noise. There's more to communication than tossing words out into the world.

Have you ever offended someone because they misunderstood what you said? We like to think that we are only responsible for our intentions, but that simply isn't true. Or at least, it's not true for anyone who is interested in being a successful person with strong working relationships.

Before you communicate, remember two things:

1. Communication is only complete when the message sent equals the message received.

2. Communication is the responsibility of the sender.

This means your role in communication just increased immensely.

With this understanding, communication requires you to have a good knowledge of your audience so that you can anticipate how your message may be received. Consider potential ways that your message could be misunderstood and how to avoid them. Remember your audience's triggers. Learn to think before you speak. The time it takes to communicate carefully will be repaid many times over as you avoid costly miscommunications.

> **You job's not done until message sent = message received.**

Remember this when you're trying to show yourself trustworthy by working the Trust Model. Your job's not done until the message you're trying to send (of integrity, competence, or compassion) is fully received. If trust is low, find the weak spot in the three-legged stool. If you've already been demonstrating that characteristic, dig a bit deeper until you find the disconnect. Maybe you just need to keep working at it over time, or maybe you'll discover a breakdown in communication. Perhaps something you thought you were communicating, such as recognition for the other person's contributions (a sign of your compassion), wasn't getting through. Or, a habit you weren't aware of (like a propensity to interrupt when someone else is speaking) was communicating something you never intended.

Take responsibility for your communication, and make it your mission that message sent equals message received.

A MATTER OF GIVE-AND-GIVE

Like most things that are worth doing, building trust is not a matter of give-and-take, but of give-and-give.

Say you've offered trust and tried to demonstrate the elements of the Trust Model, but the other person hasn't responded with trust in return. Are you off the hook? You did your part, they didn't do theirs, so what happens to the relationship is no longer your responsibility, right?

The problem is that after that first step, you stood back with your old friend the scorecard, waiting for the other person to act. You resumed your role as the fairness referee. When the other person didn't act, you got frustrated. After a few rounds of this, you started feeling ill used and bitter.

If all you care about is being right, fine. But if you want more—if you actually want to win at the relationship and build a high-trust team, you'll have to go further. A lot further. In fact, you have to stop keeping track of how far you've gone and just keep moving forward, as long as it takes.

When I speak to groups about trust, I will often pick out a random guy from the back row, make everyone look at him, and tell the group that he had done something to offend me and upset me. I offer my forgiveness to the person in front of everyone, and then I ask the group what I need to do if I want to move towards him. If he is going to do nothing but sit there, but I want to be in relationship, what must I do?

"Take a step," the group says. I take a step. We're still pretty far apart. "Now what?" "Take another step." The other guy, usually embarrassed that I called him out, sinks lower in his chair. "Now what?" "Take another step." "He's not moving towards me. What do I need to do?" "Take another step." No matter how many times I ask the question, there is only ever one thing to do: take a step forward. It's awkward and it takes a long time, but one step at a time I walk to the back of the room. The awkwardness is intentional, because that's exactly what it feels like to keep offering trust when it's not returned.

If you're in the habit of getting offended when you make an effort and the other person doesn't respond in kind, stop. The "no good deed goes unpunished" sentiment is rooted in selfishness and arrogance and a victim mindset, and it will get you nowhere. Do yourself a favor and remove it from your vocabulary.

> **Leaders never give fifty percent and then sit back in the comfortable knowledge that they did their part.**

Leaders never give fifty percent and then sit back in the comfortable knowledge that they did their part. The person who wants high-trust relationships must be willing to give one hundred percent indefinitely.

Whether you see results in two days or two hundred, keep giving trust and demonstrating the Trust Model. Don't fall back into keeping score of the other person's response. You worry about your role. Keep walking towards the other person, one awkward step at a time, until you reach your goal.

LAY DOWN YOUR RIGHTS

The fight for trust really comes down to one decision: Are you more concerned with insisting on your rights or taking ownership? Will you insist on your right to withhold trust until it's earned, even if doing so prevents you from having a high-trust relationship? Or will you take the responsibility both to give unearned trust and to use the Trust Model to show yourself trustworthy to others?

RIGHTS AND RESPONSIBILITIES

The interesting thing about rights and responsibilities is that you can't have both. If you are going to take the responsibilities of a true leader, you won't be able to insist on your rights.

When we start out brand spanking new in an entry-level job, we have all sorts of rights. We have the right to make a mistake, and maybe even the expectation of it. We have the right to expect that we'll be given the tools and resources and training to do our jobs. We have the right to a lunch break or to call in sick or to take vacation when we want to. We can leave work when the clock hits five. And we certainly have the right to avoid late night board meetings or working on the weekends without comp time.

A funny thing happens as responsibility increases. All those rights disappear one by one. The higher you are in an organization, the fewer rights people have. Oh, they may have more freedoms—like the ability to take a two-hour lunch when they want to—but that's usually because they've exchanged the right to be paid for their time for the responsibility of being paid for the results that they achieve, no matter how much work it takes. They carry responsibility for profit and loss, a budget, and the results of other people's work. They are answerable for making the workplace safe and for their employees' general welfare. Their behavior reflects on the company seven days a week. They are never off duty.

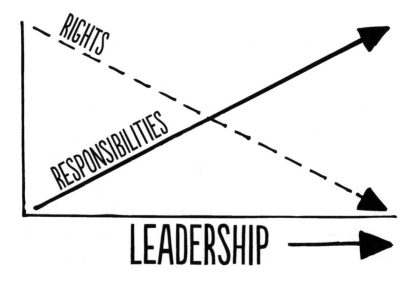

It's like this simple line graph. The higher your level of leadership, the fewer rights and the more responsibilities you have. The two things have an inverse relationship to one another.

You could also replace "leadership" with "trust." As trust increases, rights go down and responsibilities go up.

Most of the time we think about this phenomenon as the progression from entry-level to executive level, like I just described. An entry-level employee would be at the left of the graph, and a CEO would be at the right. But the powerful thing about this concept is that it's not limited by a formal title or job role. Employees at the lowest level can grasp this principle, surrender their rights, and lead with high influence and trust, and CEOs at the top of their companies can ignore it, insist on their rights, and lose their influence. It's more about the leadership you take than the position you have.

Leaders who put their rights above their responsibilities are positional leaders. They rely on the authority of their title to push people around. They demand trust as a right, but rarely give it in return.

Leaders who lay down their rights for their responsibilities are servant leaders. They get underneath their teams and lift them up. They make less of themselves and more of others. Their teams trust them happily, because integrity, competence, and compassion come out in everything they do. It's not that they let themselves be pushed around or taken advantage of. They lay down their rights out of strength and courage. They serve their teams to make them more effective, efficient, and just plain better every day. Great leaders are servant leaders.

The Lift Team

Over the past year I have had the privilege of seeing the rights-and-responsibilities principle at work in a new way. In 2012 my family got to be a part of starting a new church in our city. During the months before the first Sunday service there was a group of people who came together to be part of the church plant. The pastor called us the Lift Team.

I didn't think too much of the term at first. A lot of churches these days are all about their trendy names and image, so I thought this was just another cool way to hype up a not-so-cool thing: we were the people who loaded the equipment into our rented space each week, picked up trash afterwards, or watched the kids in the nursery. Not very glamorous.

But then something happened. I watched the pastors as they led this church and developed the Lift Team. I watched how they invested in people and how their words, their vision, and their actions were aligned. They had grasped something real.

One day, my pastor shared what "Lift Team" means to him and why he chose that name instead of calling it a leadership team or a ministry team. He said, "We are not here to lead people, to be volunteers, or to do the ministry of this church for everyone else. We are here to get low so that we can get under the people of this church and lift them up so that they can do the work that God has called them to do."

This is exactly the kind of humility that wins high trust. I don't know what you think of churches, church plants, or ministry teams. That's not the point. But I am very curious what you think about being a part of a Lift Team.

It is not the function of good leaders to do the work of their teams for them, nor to trail blaze ahead and hope that someone follows. It is the function of great leaders to get under their teams and lift them up so that they can be the best they can be.

Is your team a Lift Team? Do you think of your job as more important than your team's jobs, or do you consider it your role to lift them up, make them better, and empower them to excel? Do you consider it your duty as a leader to serve, humble yourself, give trust, demonstrate trust, and take responsibility for the wellbeing of your team? If so, then you will have no problem developing your people into a high-trust team.

When we voluntarily sacrifice our rights and accept the responsibility to lead our teams from below, we are servant leaders, high-trust leaders, and official members of a Lift Team.

THE CONTINUUM OF TRUST

There's an old saying that trust takes a lifetime to earn and an instant to lose. That makes me tired just thinking about it! Why would anyone put in the hard work to build trust if it takes forever and could disappear with the smallest mistake?

Thankfully, trust isn't all or nothing. There is a continuum of trust. No matter how new a relationship is, or what kind of negative experiences both parties have had in the past, every one of your relationships is somewhere on the trust continuum. You may be at a three when you want to be at a seven, or a six when you want to be at a ten, but very few of us are at zero. No matter where you are, just work the Trust Model and you'll see progress.

And, on the other side, trust isn't usually lost in an instant from one mistake. Established trust is strong enough to withstand minor misunderstandings, and even after a more significant offense, trust is not usually damaged beyond repair. Find the break, acknowledge the problem, and take one step at a time in the right direction.

If you get discouraged about how far you have to go to have high-trust relationships, keep this image of a continuum in mind. You don't have to jump from a one to a ten. You simply have to make progress. When people see your consistency in making those small steps, that "long way to go" actually works in your favor. Your very perseverance reinforces people's confidence in your integrity, your commitment to competence, and your compassion.

"JUST TRUST ME" IS A FOUR-LETTER WORD

No matter how good a person you are, and regardless of your professional track record or achievements, you don't have a trump card that gives you the right to automatic trust from your team. You can't force anyone to trust you. You can only be responsible for your part: giving trust and demonstrating the Trust Model. The other person ultimately needs to choose to trust you. Don't try to manipulate or coerce. Be patient.

I am my children's father. That entitles me to certain things, but automatic trust isn't one of them. If I want to raise the level of trust that exists between me and my boys, I need to find out where the breakdown is and do what I can to fix it. I am my employees' boss. I could use my position manipulatively and try to demand trust. But if I'm wise, I won't. Instead of insisting on what is due me, I need to listen, ask questions, and respond with my actions. No leader is above the need to demonstrate their integrity, competence, and compassion when they want to win high-trust relationships.

Start to consider the phrase "just trust me" a four-letter word. It should only ever be said as a last resort. In saying those words, you're cashing in on the relational equity you've built with a person. Reserve it for the rarest of occasions.

TAKE A STEP OF
FAITH

There's a big difference between belief and faith. Believing these principles work and having the faith to use them are not the same thing. It's easy to say you believe a bulletproof vest works. Faith is being willing to put it on and take a bullet.

Once you decide that you want high trust for you and your team, put that desire into action. Will you stand with me and demonstrate your faith in these principles, your faith in others, and your faith in yourself?

If not now, then when?
If not you, then who?

Write down the names of one or more people with whom you want higher trust. For each person, think of one thing you can do to give trust, and do those things this week.

I've read stacks of books on leadership, teams, personal growth, you name it. I can highlight and underline inspiring sentences with the best of them. But highlighted words won't do a thing to make lasting change in our lives or relationship.

If you want to take steps towards higher trust, why not start now? Are you planning to wait until you feel ready? Are you hoping to find a magical moment where the stars align and everyone to whom you need to offer trust is ready to receive it? That moment will never come. Act anyway.

Do something small to build trust today. If the time is not now, then when will it ever be? And if you aren't the person to do it, then who is? The time is now. We can't change the past, we can't predict the future, but we can act in the present.

Make a list of people you may have offended. Add to it people with whom you may not have communicated as clearly as possible. Then add people with whom you keep hitting relational walls and have a low Trust Factor. Each day pick one or two people from the list to reach out to in one of the following ways:

- Choose one practical way to give trust from the list at the end of Trustology 101, and do it.

- Seek feedback from someone on your list regarding your leadership blind spots—what you may be unintentionally communicating, or ways you may have frustrated or hurt them.

- Squint with your ears. In other words, listen carefully. Humble yourself and hear each person's feedback. Don't respond or defend yourself when they bring up a criticism.

- Ask each person to forgive you for your past behaviors and actions.

- Ask them to give you one or two examples of ways that you can improve, and then do exactly what they say.

- Provide unsolicited, sincere encouragement to each person on your team. Explain what you appreciate about them, how you value them, and what good you see in them.

- Learn what drives them. What are they most interested in? What do they care about? Then make time to talk with them about these things.

- Figure out what about each person bugs you or frustrates you. Then, determine what you own in that frustration. Are you holding them to unspoken expectations you haven't communicated? Have you dropped the ball on follow-up or development in the past? Ask yourself how you can be part of the solution.

There will always be excuses to put off taking action. But if not now, then when? If not you, then who?

Discovery Questions

How high is the Trust Factor in your key relationships? How could you work the Trust Model to improve it?

What kind of feedback do you routinely get from your friends, family members, and coworkers? How could you respond to that feedback in a way that builds trust?

With whom do the messages you send not equal the ones that are received? What do you know about those people that would help you understand how they're hearing you? How can you communicate your intentions more clearly?

TRUSTOLOGY 301:
LEADING
HIGH-TRUST
TEAMS

HOW TO USE TRUSTOLOGY 301

By now you understand that giving trust is your responsibility, no matter what the other person does in return. You also know how to increase trust by using the principles of the Trust Model's three-legged stool. In this final section, we'll look at how to lead your group to become a high-trust team.

When Peak Solutions works with clients to identify and address a problem in their organization, we lead them through a proven process of discovery to a place where they can decide how to move forward.

Trustology 301 is structured around the four stages of that process:

1. Assess your team

2. Define the gaps

3. Examine the issues

4. Make a game plan

This is the same process I've shared with hundreds of clients, with concrete, measurable results. Take your team through this journey and you will be on your way to having a high-trust, high-performance team.

ASSESS YOUR TEAM

TAKE YOUR TEMPERATURE

Assessing your team is about taking the temperature of your group to find out where you are beginning and how far you have to go to develop a high-trust team. How much trust does your team already have with each other? What are the major roadblocks and

Prescription without diagnosis is malpractice.

debris that you'll have to clear before you can move forward? Take your time with this stage, because this is where you'll get to see how things look from your team's perspective. The information that emerges might surprise you, but be open to those surprises. If you don't get accurate feedback now, all your efforts in the rest of the stages will be like shooting in the dark. Without the right diagnosis, you could end up taking a lot of the wrong kind of medicine without it doing anybody any good. Prescription without diagnosis is malpractice. Use this stage to get a full assessment of your team's current situation.

When I'm working with teams, I often start out having each member do a Trust Factor assessment. They take the questionnaire once about how they believe the team is doing as a whole, and again about how they think others perceive them. The two questionnaires are given in the pages that follow. The purpose of this assessment is to find out what your team members believe about the group's current strengths and weaknesses in each of the three areas of the Trust Model.

First, before you ask your team to take this assessment, take it yourself. You can take both questionnaires in the context of the team that you lead or the team that you are a part of, or both.

When you draw your team together to take the assessment, begin by casting the vision for high-trust teams. Explain where you want to take them and why. Talk about the benefits of high trust and the costs of low trust. Strongly encourage your team members to be as candid and honest as possible as they answer the questions. Now is not the time to spare feelings. Now is the time to identify problems so that you can find solutions and make a better future.

THE TRUST FACTOR ASSESSMENT FOR TEAMS

Using the scale below, assess how true you think each statement is of your team as a whole.

1 - Almost Never   2 - Seldom   3 - Sometimes   4 - Often   5 - Almost Always

Do the members of your team:

1 2 3 4 5   "Walk the talk" and live out your organization's mission and values?

1 2 3 4 5   Have clear and unambiguous goals, values, and commitments that everyone understands?

1 2 3 4 5   Comply with legal business regulations and company policies and help each other do the same?

1 2 3 4 5   Never cut corners or stretch the truth concerning policies, procedures, and rules?

1 2 3 4 5   Act from a well-defined set of guiding principles?

1 2 3 4 5   Do what they say they will do?

1 2 3 4 5   Accept accountability rather than place blame when things go wrong?

1 2 3 4 5   Arrive on time for meetings?

1 2 3 4 5   Have consistency and predictability in their behavior and performance?

1 2 3 4 5   Deal honestly with one another, other teams at the company, vendors, and customers?

_____ Integrity Score (sum of questions 1-10)

Do the members of your team:

1 2 3 4 5   Possess the technical expertise to do their jobs?

1 2 3 4 5   Operate under clear and unambiguous goals, values, and commitments that everyone can identify?

1 2 3 4 5   Deliver the business results they promise?

1 2 3 4 5   Have the education and/or expertise necessary for the demands of their jobs?

1 2 3 4 5   Seek to improve areas of deficiency?

1 2 3 4 5   Share their knowledge and expertise with one another and across the company?

1 2 3 4 5   Easily acquire new knowledge in areas where they don't have all the answers?

1 2 3 4 5   Help others get up to speed and grow their skills and abilities?

1 2 3 4 5   Are eager to learn something new every day?

1 2 3 4 5   Clearly understand their roles and responsibilities?

_____ Competence Score (sum of questions 11-20)

Do the members of your team:

1 2 3 4 5   Treat others with dignity and respect?

1 2 3 4 5   Have faith in everyone's ability to contribute?

1 2 3 4 5   Listen to and seek input from one another and from other teams in the company?

1 2 3 4 5   Act in a fair manner?

1 2 3 4 5   Put the good of the whole team or organization above protecting their own turf?

1 2 3 4 5   Choose to say and do the right thing when it is difficult?

1 2 3 4 5   Seek to understand before being understood?

1 2 3 4 5   Generally believe the best about others and give them the benefit of the doubt?

1 2 3 4 5   Get to know each other personally and show a genuine interest in each other's lives?

1 2 3 4 5   Willingly engage in healthy conflict when it's needed?

_____ Compassion Score (sum of questions 21-30)

_____ TOTAL TRUST FACTOR SCORE (sum of all questions)

YOUR TEAM'S TRUST FACTOR TEMPERATURE

Cold: Score of 30-60

You and your team members are in danger of alienating yourselves from each other and creating a culture of low trust. Your lack of attention to trust is short-circuiting your ability to build strong relationships and get results. You may consider asking for direct feedback from your team members about their perceptions of you. Give trust to get trust, demonstrate the three legs of the Trust Model, and stop sabotaging unity. Let others know you care to make a change and start making those changes now.

Lukewarm: Score of 61-90

Your team likely has some areas within the Trust Model that you scored well on, so focus on these areas and try to let your strengths overcome your weaknesses in other areas. It could be that team members see one another as aloof, unconcerned, and distant. The messages that you're sending aren't the messages that other team members are receiving. Try getting to know the other team members better and asking them what you can do to improve. If the team is significantly weaker in one specific leg of the Trust Model, create a sixty-day game plan on how you can change your actions and other people's perceptions of you in this area.

Warm: Score of 91-120

Your team members generally see one another as trustworthy. You manage your relationships well. Your warmth and sincerity is inviting and allows you to quickly build relationships and to ask things of each other that many teams are not able to. Evaluate the questions where you scored the highest and focus on those strengths. They are likely what draws people to your team and what gives you energy and enthusiasm. Now it is your job to help each other grow and raise your Trust Factor even higher.

Hot: Score of 121-150

You are winning the war for relationships. Consult with your colleagues to make sure their perceptions line up with yours. If they do, you likely have an extremely high amount of relational equity with these people. Consider how you can use it to become even more high performing. Keep focusing on your team, offering trust, and giving other people reason to trust you in return. Expect great things from your team.

THE TRUST FACTOR
ASSESSMENT FOR INDIVIDUALS

This time, using the scale below, assess how you think other people on your team perceive you. If you are not sure how to answer these questions, consider asking for candid feedback from a trusted member of your team.

1 - Almost Never   2 - Seldom   3 - Sometimes   4 - Often   5 - Almost Always

Would your team members say that you:

1	2	3	4	5	"Walk the talk" and live out your organization's mission and values?
1	2	3	4	5	Operate under clear and unambiguous goals, values, and commitments that your team can identify?
1	2	3	4	5	Comply with legal business regulations and company policies and help others do the same?
1	2	3	4	5	Do not cut corners or stretch the truth concerning policies, procedures, and rules?
1	2	3	4	5	Act from a well-defined set of guiding principles?
1	2	3	4	5	Do what you say you will do?
1	2	3	4	5	Accept accountability rather than place blame when things go wrong?
1	2	3	4	5	Arrive on time for meetings?
1	2	3	4	5	Have consistency in your character between who you are at home, at work, and at play?
1	2	3	4	5	Are honest in your dealings with coworkers, customers, and vendors?

_____ Integrity Score (sum of questions 1-10)

Would your team members say that you:

1	2	3	4	5	Possess the technical expertise to do your job?

1	2	3	4	5	Set clear goals and objectives for yourself and others?
1	2	3	4	5	Deliver the business results you promise?
1	2	3	4	5	Have the education and/or expertise necessary for the demands of your job?
1	2	3	4	5	Seek to improve areas of deficiency?
1	2	3	4	5	Share your knowledge and expertise with your team and other teams across the company?
1	2	3	4	5	Easily acquire new knowledge in areas where you don't have all the answers?
1	2	3	4	5	Help others get up to speed and grow their skills and abilities?
1	2	3	4	5	Are eager to learn something new every day?
1	2	3	4	5	Understand your role and responsibilities?

_____ Competence Score (sum of questions 11-20)

Would your team members say that you:

1	2	3	4	5	Treat others with dignity and respect?
1	2	3	4	5	Have faith in everyone's ability to contribute?
1	2	3	4	5	Listen to and seek input from others?
1	2	3	4	5	Act in a fair manner?
1	2	3	4	5	Put the good of the whole team above protecting your turf?
1	2	3	4	5	Choose to say and do the difficult thing when it is right to do so?
1	2	3	4	5	Seek to understand before being understood?
1	2	3	4	5	Generally believe the best about others and give them the benefit of the doubt?
1	2	3	4	5	Get to know your team members personally and show a genuine interest in their lives?
1	2	3	4	5	Willingly engage in healthy conflict when it's needed?

_____ Compassion Score (sum of questions 21-30)

_____TOTAL TRUST FACTOR SCORE (sum of all questions)

YOUR TRUST FACTOR TEMPERATURE

Cold: Score of 30-60

You are in danger of alienating yourself and creating a culture of low trust in your team. Your lack of attention to trust is short-circuiting your ability to build strong relationships and get results from others. You may consider asking for direct feedback from your team members about their perceptions of you. Give trust to get trust, demonstrate the three legs of the Trust Model, and stop sabotaging unity. Let others know you care to make a change and start making those changes now.

Lukewarm: Score of 61-90

You likely have some areas within the Trust Model that you scored well on, so focus on these areas and try to let your strengths overcome your weaknesses in other areas. It could be that others see you as aloof, unconcerned, and distant. The messages that you're sending aren't the messages that the team is receiving. Try getting to know your team members better and asking them what you can do to improve. If you are significantly weaker in one specific leg of the Trust Model, create a sixty-day game plan on how to change your actions and other people's perceptions of you in this area.

Warm: Score of 91-120

You are generally seen as trustworthy. You manage yourself and your relationships with others well. Your warm and sincere personality is inviting and allows you to build relationships quickly and to ask things of people that others are not able to. Evaluate the questions where you scored the highest and focus on those strengths. They are likely what draws people to you and what gives you energy and enthusiasm. Now it is your job to help others grow and increase their own Trust Factor.

Hot: Score of 121-150

You are winning the war for relationships. Consult with your colleagues to make sure their perceptions of you line up with your perceptions of yourself. If they do, you likely have an extremely high amount of relational equity built up with your team. Consider how you can use the trust you have to make your team even more high performing. Keep focusing on your team members, offering trust to one another, and giving them reason to trust you in return. Expect great things from your team.

INTERPRETING THE TRUST FACTOR ASSESSMENT

TAKING THE ASSESSMENT

There are many ways to gather and discuss the feedback from this assessment. If your team isn't mature or high performing enough to have every member complete the assessment, you and a few key members could take it on behalf of the group. If your team is high performing and has at least a reasonable amount of maturity and willingness to improve, give the assessment to everyone.

In the interest of receiving the most honest feedback, you could have people complete the surveys anonymously and have one central person tabulate the scores. An online version of this assessment is also available, which allows teams to give anonymous feedback and provides the leader with a complete report on how their team perceives their overall Trust Factor.

REVIEWING THE RESULTS

Once your team has taken both versions of the assessment, make note of the results. The first third of the questions relate to integrity, the second to competence, and the third to compassion. Do any themes emerge from your team?

If one person rated the team's Trust Factor at a 50, and another team member gave it a 150, that doesn't average out to 100. That discrepancy is a red flag indicating that something is going on that you need to pay attention to. Maybe there is a breakdown somewhere along the line of communication, where message sent does not equal message received, or maybe there is some kind of division, cliques, or gossip happening within the team. Maybe some people are privy to knowledge that the others are not, or perhaps the outlier response comes from someone who is projecting their personal biases and past experiences onto the team. Regardless of the reason, if your team rates the trust level low, there are offenses and frustrations that must be dealt with.

On the other hand, if your team rated your Trust Factor really high, wonderful! Congratulate them and spend time finding out why they believe it is so high and how the team can keep it that way. High trust doesn't come without continued attention and effort, so talk about how you can maintain and even increase it.

On the self-assessments, did anyone vastly over- or under-estimate how trustworthy they appear to others? If people underestimate their own trustworthiness, give positive feedback about how you perceive their integrity, competence, and compassion. If they overestimate themselves and they're actually not doing as well as they think they are, some gentle honesty may be called for.

DEBRIEFING AS A TEAM

No matter how you gather the data, whether by sampling a few people or by giving the assessment to everyone, it is important to get your whole team together to discuss the findings of the survey. The best results usually come from discussions with a full team.

When you gather, the team leader or a respected peer on the team can share the findings with the rest of the group and ask some open-ended questions.

- What do these results tell us about our team?
- What of these results are good?
- What of these results are not good?
- How is a lack of trust affecting our team?
- What are the most critical areas that we should address right away?
- What are the characteristics of a low-trust environment?
- What are the consequences of having low trust?
- What are the characteristics of a high-trust environment?
- What are the payoffs of high trust?
- What makes trust more elusive today than in the past?
- What business situations make trust more difficult?

Make a time for each member to share their answers to the questions. Create a safe environment and don't discount anyone's feedback. Do not allow personal attacks. If someone brings up a specific person, direct their comments to facts and the problem versus emotions and the person. Listen carefully to find out what was behind the team's responses. What do they see as the systemic weaknesses in the organization? What is keeping them from having high trust in the group?

This is the time to gather as much rich, layered data as possible, so that you can get the best diagnosis before you move forward.

BREAKING THE STALEMATE
USING THE TRUST MODEL TO DIAGNOSE YOUR HESITATION TO TRUST

Before we move on to the next stage of becoming a high-trust team, I want to mention one other way to use the Trust Factor assessment: to help you diagnose why you find it difficult to trust a specific person.

When you find yourself reluctant to give specific people increased responsibility, or to entrust them with a big project, or to be vulnerable, do you always know why you're hesitating? I don't. Usually in that kind of situation I just feel stuck. I know that trust must be given, not earned, but for some reason I feel uncomfortable trusting this person. This situation is a trust stalemate.

The key to breaking through a trust stalemate is to deal in specifics, not ambiguous generalities. We need to stop saying "I don't trust so-and-so." That statement is vague and unhelpful. It offends without giving any direction. Or, put yourself on the other side of the conversation. When someone says to you, "I'm sorry, I just don't trust you," are you left feeling empowered, with a clear idea of how to fix the problem? Probably not. You feel stuck.

Instead of saying that we just don't trust someone, we need to train ourselves to identify the source of the mistrust:

- I lack confidence in their *integrity*.

- I doubt their *competence* for this job.

- I don't sense their *compassion* for others.

Identifying which one of the three legs of our trust stool is missing or weak is the first step towards breaking a trust stalemate. Once we have that knowledge, we can do several things with it.

> **We need to stop saying "I don't trust so-and-so." That statement is vague and unhelpful.**

We may choose to still give trust despite our hesitations, but now we'll be doing it with our eyes wide open.

Other times, we'll choose to have healthy conflict with the other person about the cause of our hesitation, leading to renewed trust in the future.

And even in the times that we ultimately decide not to trust the person with the opportunity in question, we will come away wiser for identifying the root problem.

To diagnose a hesitation to trust, take the Trust Factor assessment again, but this time, answer the questions about the person you hesitate to trust. How well do you think the assessment statements describe them? The first third of the questions relate to integrity, the second third to competence, and the final third to compassion. Is the score for one of those three areas significantly lower than the others? Does that discovery give any further clarity about how you can take steps to address the problem?

By identifying the source of mistrust, you'll break the trust stalemate and be one step closer to rebuilding trust.

DEFINE THE GAPS

HOW FAR FROM HERE TO THERE?

After you assess your team, the next step in building a high-trust team is to define the gaps: to delineate, based on the results from the Trust Factor assessment and feedback from team members, what the gaps are between where you want to be and where you are now, and to determine what you ultimately aspire to for your team.

> **trust gap:** the difference between where you would like to be as a team and where you are right now; the root problems that keep you from functioning as a high-trust, high-performance team

For instance, if your team assessments said that employees don't believe that the company cares about its employees, or that people are more focused on their own areas of responsibility than on the enterprise or team as a whole, that would show a gap in perceived compassion. As long as that gap exists, you won't be able to develop as a high-trust team.

Other examples of gaps include:

GAPS OF INTEGRITY

- Not following through on commitments
- Asking team members to do things that are not in their best interests or those of the company
- Placing blame, disowning responsibility, and generally living below the line
- A lack of honest, open communication
- Politics, silos, and turf protection
- Arbitrary goals (if any) and no clear direction for team members
- Not honoring people's time and resources by stealing or poorly managing either one

GAPS OF COMPETENCE

- An unwillingness on the part of team members to share information or expertise with associates
- A skill and knowledge gap that slows down and inhibits the team
- Frequently failing to meet goals and objectives
- A lack of personal growth or desire to improve

- Active hoarding of knowledge and skills to maintain power and relevance

GAPS OF COMPASSION

- Treating people like tools or resources to get things done
- Not listening to what people are saying and how they are feeling
- Cynicism and lack of care for others
- No desire or effort to understand others and where they are coming from
- Selfishness and lack of team unity
- Greater focus on me than we

Using the team's assessment results as a conversation starter, invite team members to help you define the gaps between where you are and where you want to be.

OWN THE GAPS

Once you have identified the gaps, two things are critical: you must get agreement on the gaps from your team and everyone must take ownership of the gaps. The gaps aren't bad; doing nothing about them is.

Discuss the gaps with your team until everyone has a clear idea of what they are. Agreement here is important, because if someone feels left out of this process, it will be hard to get buy-in later when it's time to come up with solutions.

Once you have agreement, everyone must take ownership of the gaps—even ones they don't think they're responsible for or aren't bothered by.

YOUR PROBLEMS ARE MY PROBLEMS

Sometimes we refuse to take ownership of a gap that someone else identified because we don't think it's really that big of a deal, or at least we think there are other gaps that should be addressed first.

It drives my colleague Jake crazy when I'm inattentive to time when we travel, or when technology doesn't work as it should during a workshop. Those things don't get under my skin in the same way, but I'd be pretty arrogant and selfish if I dismissed his concerns just because they weren't the same as mine.

Caring about what other people care about is a basic part of maturity. Saying, "I know this thing bothers you, but it doesn't bother me, so I really don't care," is saying that you don't respect or value that person as an independent human being. As you talk about gaps with your team, set the ground rule that you take everyone's concerns seriously.

GET A CPA

Another reason that we often reject ownership of a gap is because we think it's someone else's fault. "Sure, there may have been a quality control issue with our product recently, but the guys in Operations were to blame." "Making sure clients are satisfied is the account representative's job, not mine."

I once worked with a client where everyone in the team had been aware, to one level or another, of a major problem with a client's order, but no one had been willing to call it out or do something to fix it. Quality knew the product was bad, Sales knew the product was bad, Operations knew the product was bad, and the management team knew the product was bad—but the company shipped it anyway. It was a textbook case of lack of ownership.

I often start out the first day of a new training program by announcing that we're going to give all of the attendees their very own CPA. (This gets an especially excited reaction around tax time.) They soon find out, when we fail to pull a few hundred certified public accountants out of our briefcases, that we're talking about a different kind of CPA.

CPA is a mindset of personal accountability and responsibility. It says that in every problem you face, you either:

- Cause the problem
- Participate in the problem
- Allow the problem to happen

As you face your gaps as a team, everyone must take ownership of all the gaps. Even if one person didn't cause the quality issue or drop the ball with a client, everyone needs to take responsibility for the problem and the solution.

IT'S NOT ABOUT THE COFFEE

Several years ago during a leadership development session I had one of my most memorable debates of all time. One of the leaders in the group was a guy named Mike, the manager of one of my client's locations. Mike was a seasoned employee who had worked for the company for over twenty years and had a great deal of industry expertise.

We were talking about harmful behaviors in the workplace and how to turn people and their bad behaviors around. Mike told the group about a real-life scenario where he badly wanted to see change. He explained how he had an employee who was disrespectful and disregarded authority. I asked for specific examples, to which Mike sheepishly said that his troubled employee refused to make more coffee after he took the last cup. Not every now and then, but every day. Sometimes several times in the same day.

Now, don't get me wrong, I appreciate the tragedy of an empty coffee pot, but it seemed a bit far-fetched to call this a "harmful behavior." Not wanting to minimize Mike's challenge, I probed a bit deeper. Surely there was more to the situation.

> **The root of our problems is usually something we're contributing to.**

"What seems like no big deal is a really big deal to me," he said. "Every single time this guy takes the last cup of coffee and doesn't make a new pot, he is ruining things around here."

"Ruining things?" I asked.

"Yes, he is making everyone miserable, including me," Mike barked.

"What do you think is the root of your anger and frustration, Mike?" I asked. What I was really asking him was, "Where is the real gap here? What is the underlying issue behind this behavior?"

I asked Mike, "Are there other things going on with this guy that make the empty coffee pot a bigger issue?" After some dialogue, it turned out that this employee was doing more than just not making the coffee. Mike mentioned his disrespect for fellow employees and his shortness with the customers. This employee not only had a lack of respect for his manager, he was downright selfish and crabby. Mike's fixation on the coffee had kept him from seeing the root issue.

After this dialogue I thought that Mike would see the wider problem and be willing to address it, so I asked, "Now Mike, what do you think is the real issue here? Do you see a bigger problem?"

After all of our discussion, Mike simply said, "Yeah, I see the problem. He won't make the coffee and he is a selfish jerk."

"Is that the root of his problem?"

"Yep, he won't make the coffee."

Frustrated and at a bit of a loss I shouted, "IT'S NOT ABOUT THE COFFEE, MIKE!"

The coffee was a symptom, an overflow of other things, but the coffee wasn't the problem. All Mike's colleagues agreed, and over the next fifteen minutes they helped me share that the real issue was the employee's lack of respect and disregard for authority and Mike's poor communication about expectations and boundaries.

How many times are we in situations where we keep complaining about the coffee when, in reality, *it's not about the coffee!* We focus on the most annoying symptom of the problem instead of the problem itself. (I suspect that's because the bigger problem is usually something we're contributing to. Remember CPA? We either cause a problem, participate in a problem, or allow it to happen. Facing the real issue makes us face our own shortcomings as leaders, and that's uncomfortable.) In Mike's case, his pent-up frustration about the coffee was keeping him from taking an honest look at how his leadership, or lack thereof, had been contributing to the problem.

As you're determining the gaps in your team's Trust Factor, look past the surface issues. The presenting symptom might be obvious, but it's likely that the root is buried a few layers deeper.

Two weeks after this conversation with Mike, a book arrived in my mailbox. It was titled *It's Not About the Coffee: Leadership Principles from a Life at Starbucks.* The book was from one of Mike's colleagues. I laughed out loud.

TENSION IS YOUR FRIEND

As you are defining the gaps in your team, you might find that some of them are related to the tension between two opposing values, like work and family, grace and truth, or micromanagement and empowerment. When it comes to classic dilemmas like these, keep in mind that not all problems have solutions. Some are just tensions that need to be managed.

When you hear the word *tension*, what comes to mind? Awkward conversations? Passive-aggressive conflict? Neck pain? The truth is that tension is not necessarily a bad thing. In fact, nothing on earth works without tension between opposing forces.

Your car couldn't move without the opposing pressures of pistons and combustion putting tension on the drivetrain, making your axle rotate and your car move forward. Friction on the road allows the driver to control the car. Eliminate friction, as when ice covers a road, and you have a mess on your hands.

At the gym you only get stronger when there's enough resistance against your muscles to create stress, causing the muscle fibers to tear and heal back denser and stronger.

Birds, kites, and planes soar because of tension between the forces of lift, gravity, thrust, and drag. Pilots can control an airplane in flight only because there is the perfect amount of tension between aerodynamic lift and gravity. Too much gravity, and the plane would be stuck on the ground. Too much lift and the plane could never land.

Is this a problem that needs a solution, or merely a tension that I need to manage?

Likewise, without enough tension in our teams we would be passive and motionless. Managing opposing tensions can be what it takes to energize us, propel us forward, and initiate change. Tension is like food. Eat too much and you might be sick, but don't eat enough and you'll feel pretty uncomfortable as well.

When we are faced with challenges, a common reaction is to try to eliminate the pain or walk away from the frustration. Tensions are uncomfortable, so we don't like living there. We waste too much of our time trying to eliminate tensions that will always exist.

My first inclination when faced with a problem is to try to fix it so it goes away—typical male, I guess. This Y chromosome is obsessed with problem solving. But unfortunately for problem-solvers, not all problems have solutions.

When your team brings up an issue in this gap-defining process, ask, "Is this a problem that has or needs a solution, or a tension that we need to manage?" If it is a tension, then instead of asking "How do we solve this problem?" ask,

- Are we in balance here?
- What do the present circumstances require of us?
- How can we get into a more healthy rhythm between these two values?

As opposed to problems, tensions actually make us better, more productive, and more intentional. Our goal when we feel stretched between opposing drives and desires should not be to eliminate the tensions but to walk a healthy line between them.

In the conflict between family and work, for example, don't expect to arrive at a place where those two areas of life are no longer in tension with each other. They always will be, and that's a good thing. The tension makes us better.

Likewise, leaders are often pulled between our desire to lead and empower our teams and our tendency to micromanage in order to control quality output. Both empowerment and quality are important. If we abandon either, we won't be good at our jobs.

In our relationships, we desire peace, but the paradox is that we can sometimes only win more peaceful relationships by embracing healthy conflict. On the other hand, we don't want to nag. There is no way to resolve that tension—it will always exist in any relationship that's deep enough to have conflict. We can only hold both impulses in hand and do our best to manage the tension.

Andy Stanley, speaking to this topic in his teaching "The Upside of Tension," says that there is a prevalent myth that the best leaders, managers, and organizations solve all their problems and resolve all their tensions. But, he says, that's not true. The truth is that the best leaders don't resolve all of the tensions. They learn how to use the necessary tension in organizational life for the sake of progress. Every organization, therefore, has problems that shouldn't be solved. Stanley says, "Progress depends not on the resolution of those tensions but on the successful management of those tensions."

So how do we discern between problems to solve and tensions to manage? Stanley offers three questions to ask:

Does this problem or tension keep resurfacing? If a problem keeps coming up again and again, that's a tension that needs to be managed. For example, our clients in the agriculture industry face great seasonal challenges. Planting season is short, growing season is short, and harvest season is short. Our clients can't support heavy staffing all year long, but they never have enough labor to meet the demands of these short yet busy seasons. This cycle is complicated by unpredictable weather and other elements that are out of their control. This is an ongoing tension without an easy answer, and one that they'll have to figure out a way to manage every year.

> **Every organization has problems that shouldn't be solved.**

Are there mature advocates on both sides of the issue? If there are respected people on both sides of a debate, there probably isn't a black or white solution. For instance, imagine that one of your team members consistently seeks to minimize risk and wants to limit market exposure, while another is typically more open to risks and desires to enter new markets. Neither is wrong, so you'll need to keep both voices in mind.

Are the two sides of the tension interdependent? When a conflict represents two sides of the same coin, the tension between them is probably necessary and even helpful. An example of this is the tension between work and family. If you gave either side all your time, you'd lose the other side entirely. The tension between them is helpful because it helps you make the most of your time in both areas.

As you work to define your gaps, don't get mired down trying to resolve unresolvable tensions. Instead, identify them, brainstorm how you can get into a healthier rhythm, and communicate to your team the expectation that because these are tensions that will always need to be managed, the discussion is one that you can feel free to return to as needed in the future.

EXAMINE
THE
ISSUES

THE ISSUES BEHIND THE GAPS

The third step to forming a high-trust team is to examine the issues. In the context of your team's trust gaps, there are three things that every leader must seek to understand:

1. The issue

2. Their issue

3. Your issue

Defining the gaps was about understanding the gaps in your team that keep you from functioning on a high-trust level. But once you understand *the* issue, you need to take the time to understand *their* issue and *your* issue.

Understanding Their Issue

Understanding *their* issues is about seeking to know your team, who they are, how they operate, what makes them tick, what drives them crazy, what kind of assumptions they're starting from, and how all of that affects how they understand and contribute to your trust gaps. You won't be able to understand your team's root issues, or develop a plan to address them, until you understand your team itself.

This section explores a handful of concepts that will help you gain insight into your team, including:

- How to use the DISC profile

- How to understand someone's starting line

- How to have healthy conflict

- The single most important choice that your team can make: to presume that other people have positive intentions

Use these tools as they are helpful, or use your own approaches. The point of this section is, in one way or another, to understand your team and how they are involved in the gaps that you've found.

Understanding Your Issue

Once you understand your team, it's time to take a hard look inward and examine *your* issue: the role that you've played in causing the gaps, participating in the gaps, or allowing the gaps to exist. We'll talk about how much information we can gain by taking an honest look in the mirror.

THE DISC AS A TRUST TOOL

Personality tests are psychometric tools designed to explain behavior, analyze strengths and weaknesses, and determine aptitude. I've seen some people go overboard with them, while others dismiss them as subjective and stereotypical. They are not the final word in organizational development, but I generally find them to be a beneficial tool for a leader's arsenal, especially when participants receive coaching in how to apply the results.

The reason I'm such a big fan of personality assessments is their ability to shed light on interpersonal relationships and communication. I'm less interested in knowing what "type" I am for my own sake and more interested in knowing my and my team's potential strengths and weaknesses when we interact together.

When choosing a test to use in team contexts, I have three criteria:

- I like the test and believe the results.

- It is easy to interpret.

- It works (teams find it helpful).

The test I've found that best meets those criteria is the DISC profile, an open-source assessment based on the work of psychologists William Marston, Walter Clarke, and John Greier. The DISC is easy to understand, and when you learn how the combinations of people's DISC personality types work together, you have a very robust tool. It's not the most detailed personality assessment available, but I have found that some of the more elaborate ones are too complex for the average person to remember and apply. When it comes to team discussions, the DISC is my tool of choice.

The D in DISC stands for Dominant, I stands for Influencer, S stands for Steady, and C stands for Compliant/Conscientious. Everyone has a primary type and one or more secondary types. Knowing a person's DISC type can help us understand the way they're most likely to interact with others, be motivated, be irritated, measure success, etc.

The DISC test is freely available online. What I want to talk about here is how the DISC tool can be used to help you understand your team and to build trust.

Take the DISC test as a team. The test is environment-specific, so make sure to tell team members to answer questions with a work context in mind (or your volunteer organization, or whatever context your team operates in). When everyone is done taking the test, provide some coaching and interpretation on what the results mean. Go over strengths and weaknesses of each type. Share your results with each other and express to what extent you believe the results accurately describe you. Share with others the best way to communicate with you and some dos and don'ts of working with you. Mention something specific about how each member's style has been a positive contribution to the team. Talk about how you can support each person's preferred working style.

The big advantage of the DISC test is that it's simple enough that you can usually identify a person's type even without knowing their exact test results. This information can help you better understand, relate to, and work with those who are different from you. It is easier to assume the best about someone when you know that the thing that is driving you crazy about them is actually a natural side effect of their strengths. It is easier to build trust with someone when you know what they value, what they need, and what bothers them.

When you want to build trust with a D, provide clear information, be to the point, support their goals, offer leadership opportunities, provide challenging projects, encourage healthy competition, display measurable success, avoid inefficiency, and respect the person's time.

To build trust with an I, publicly recognize their achievements, show openness to their innovative ideas, encourage expressions of creativity, provide lots of personal interaction and brainstorming, support their ideas, mix up the routine, compliment them, make room for their spontaneity, and never shame them in front of other people.

With an S, you build trust when you make them comfortable, speak kindly and pleasantly, create a relaxed environment, support their feelings, confront gently and privately, affirm that you like and enjoy them, give them an area to own, seek their opinion, protect their boundaries, appreciate their loyalty, and avoid being insensitive and impatient.

You will build trust with a C when you provide precise details, give clear expectations and deadlines, praise their thoroughness, provide logical support for decisions, give them room and time to work, support their thoughts, don't throw changes on them unexpectedly, and do not publicly expose their mistakes.

Understanding someone's natural personality type can make a big difference in learning how to have positive, smooth interactions, healthy conflict, and higher trust.

GET OUT OF THE SANDBOX

Just like understanding your team's personality types can help you better relate and understand where they're coming from, so can recognizing where they are in their own social and intellectual maturity processes.

Our awareness of other people and their differences goes through a typical process as we mature, called the four levels of social awareness:

- Sandbox: Everyone thinks like me.

- Awkward: No one thinks like me.

- Enlightened: I think differently than others.

- Wisdom: We all think differently, and that is good.

If you're finding trust gaps that involve a specific person on your team and you suspect that some social immaturity may be involved, take a look at these stages and see if one of them sounds familiar. The purpose of these stages is not to box people in or make anyone else feel superior, but rather to understand where your team members are, what crisis of thought they may be facing right now, and how you can be compassionate and helpful in that process without letting them sabotage your team.

SANDBOX THINKING

Sandbox thinking is toddler thinking. Imagine that we're looking at the average two-year-old's sandbox. Two young children are playing in the sand. Johnny has a truck. Joey wants the truck. Joey takes the truck. Johnny screams and hits Joey over the head with a plastic shovel.

In Joey's mind, taking the truck wasn't selfish. He wanted the toy, and he assumed that Johnny therefore wanted him to have the toy, too. He wasn't being selfish; he was being two. In Joey's two-year-old cognitive reasoning, he is the center of the universe. He has no concept of someone else having desires, needs, or plans that might be in conflict with his own. When Joey is hungry, he's hungry. The fact that mom desperately needs a nap or a shower or her own food doesn't even exist in his reality.

Sandbox thinking says, "Everyone thinks like me." It's selfishness, a lack of compassion, and low self-aware-

> **If a team member's social immaturity is contributing to your team's trust gaps, be compassionate and helpful without letting that person sabotage your team.**

ness. It makes the offender comes across as uncaring, demanding, and even cruel. How many times a day do we experience sandbox thinking? It's understandable in two-year-olds. It's not as easily forgiven in adults.

If you see Sandbox thinking in one of your team members, redirect them to the real problem and help them see how their actions affect others. Acknowledge their personal concerns, but remind them that it's important to consider a decision in light of its impact on the group and the direction of the company as a whole. This is a situation where tough compassion is kinder than coddling. You show that you care by helping them to move out of the center of their universe and into the playing field with everyone else.

Sometimes we can coach people out of the sandbox, sometimes we can coax them out, and sometimes we simply need to pick them up and drag them to reality.

AWKWARD THINKING

Awkward thinking is teenager thinking. If Sandbox thinking said, "Everyone thinks like me," Awkward thinking says, "No one thinks like me." Think of thirteen-year-olds who are becoming aware of themselves in a new way. They each think they are the first person in the history of the world to feel and think as they do. They believe that they think differently from their parents, their siblings, and their friends. No one understands them. They have to work hard to make their own way, create their own style, find their own music, and navigate their new culture.

In adults, Awkward thinking can be just as damaging as Sandbox thinking. Awkward-phase people come across in one of two ways. They can seem insecure, slow to act, reserved, and aloof, or they can try to protect their newfound awareness by aggressively defending their thinking and appearing arrogant, angry, and confrontational. Either way, this comes out of their belief that no one thinks like they do.

If you have team members who are stuck in this phase, help them see that they are not alone. If they're picking up on real problems, validate their frustrations. Help them realize that they are not alone in their struggles, and therefore that they can cooperate with the team to find solutions.

ENLIGHTENED THINKING

Enlightened thinking is college-student thinking. It says, "I think differently than others." Where the Awkward thinker feels isolated by their differences, the Enlightened thinker feels just that – enlightened. This is embodied by the twenty-somethings who have started to realize how the world works and where they fit in the big picture. They are navigating relationships, work, and cultural differences in a way that they haven't had to before. They are starting to see the benefit in a broader way of thinking.

At home, Enlightened thinkers spend their time trying to figure out their friends or their new spouse. They probably love personality tests! They recognize that other people have styles, approaches, and ways of thinking that are different from their own. When they interact with someone who doesn't think like them, a new level of political savvy begins to appear. They ask more questions and make fewer demands.

This is a good place to be as an adult. You are sensitive to others, you respect differences, and you try to understand why people do what they do.

Wisdom Thinking

Where the Enlightened thinker is aware of differences, the Wisdom thinker actively appreciates those differences and the contribution each person makes to the whole. This final stage says, "We all think differently, and that is good."

The Wisdom thinker is the mature individual who seeks out people with different personalities and thinking styles. Leaders in this phase intentionally hire people who think and work differently from each other to create a well-rounded team. In meetings, Wisdom thinkers ask questions not just hoping for approval but wanting pushback to strengthen their ideas.

If you aren't already in this phase, start thinking about how you can more intentionally ask for input from others who you know will approach a problem differently than you do. Expect to be strengthened by a different conclusion instead of threatened by it.

UNDERSTAND THE STARTING LINE

During a recent U.S. election cycle I came to a massive realization.

First, let me regress. My political beliefs are shaped by my worldview, and both are pretty firm. During the primaries and then the presidential election, I had many conversations, debates, and even a few arguments with people who had come to different political conclusions than I did. I was confused why they couldn't see things that seemed so clear to me, especially when they were people who I believed shared many of my values.

A few months after the election I realized something profound. I had been trying to get people to change their finish line, to join me, to be influenced to think, act, and even vote as I did. What I recognized is that it is nearly impossible to change someone's finish line without understanding where they started.

In the years since that election I have spent more time trying to understand where people are coming from, what shaped their worldview, and what their starting line was. This hasn't removed the gaps in our beliefs, but it has generated much more fruitful and less confrontational conversations.

This idea applies to so many of our human interactions. How many times do we bump into problems and get frustrated with people because we can't get them to meet us at the right finish line? The right conclusion? What if we first tried to understand where they're coming from, their starting line? That would help us understand each other better, it would increase our respect for one another, and it might help them hear our point instead of only debating it.

When you are identifying problem gaps in your team and trying to get agreement and ownership from its members, it's frustrating when another person doesn't see the problem or the solution the same way you do. As you seek to understand "their issues," try asking questions to understand where your team members are coming from:

- I'm sure you have a good reason for seeing things this way. Where are you coming from on this?

- What are the underlying values or concerns that you believe this conclusion addresses?

- Have you experienced something related to this before? What did you like or dislike about how it was handled?

- Have you found evidence to support that this conclusion is a good one?

- What do you believe is at risk here? What do you, or we, stand to lose?

- What do you, or we, stand to gain?

- Have you considered any other options?

- Are there any weaknesses to this solution as you see it?

- Are you open to another option, if it still addresses your values?

- If I had a different opinion, would you be open to hearing it?

Remember that when it comes to building trust with others, they have to have confidence in your compassion: confidence that you understand them, that you respect and value them, and that you have their best interests in mind. Whatever their conclusions, they probably have reasons for arriving at them. Try to listen before you speak, and take the time to understand the background and values that created their starting lines. And have some humility. There's a good chance your position has weaknesses, too.

It doesn't matter if you have all the facts in the world to back up your stance. If others don't believe that you care about them as people more than you care about changing their minds, they won't hear you.

Next time you can't understand someone's finish line, remember to look for their starting line.

PRESUME POSITIVE INTENT

The most vital decision you and your team can make as you seek to understand the issues behind your trust gaps (and one of the most important decisions you can make in life, period) is to assume the best about other people's intentions.

Have you noticed how we judge ourselves very differently from the way we judge others? We judge others based on their actions but ourselves based on our intentions. In the case of bad behavior, we assume that other people's mistakes reflect on their character, while we explain our own away by our circumstances. If someone cuts us off, we assume they're rude and aggressive. If we cut someone else off, it's because we were distracted by the bad day we just had. After all, we didn't *mean* to do it. If a colleagues interrupts us *again*, they must be doing it on purpose, even though we probably interrupt people all the time without noticing.

This tendency is related to a principle that is known in the field of psychology as the fundamental attribution error. Basically, it means we are too quick to assume bad things about others.

Making negative assumptions about others is a bad habit with huge relational costs, leading to misunderstandings, wasted time, hurt feelings, poor business decisions, and hoarded resources. They are probably at the root of most divorces and wars.

> **Even if you need to confront bad behavior, how much better will that conversation go if you enter into it assuming the best?**

When someone does or says something offensive to us, we are at a fork in the road. What are we going to believe about their intentions? Do they mean well or not? There are really only two options. The first is to assume that they intend to be hurtful, or are at least culpably irresponsible and inconsiderate. The second possibility is to believe that the other party has a positive intent, is doing the best that they can, and was probably operating under circumstances we didn't fully understand. In both cases it is usually just a guess, so why guess negatively?

Can you imagine how differently you would approach other people if you chose to believe the best possible option?

CHECK YOUR LENSES

Imagine that you wear sunglasses everyday. You have two pair, one with rose-tinted lenses and one with blue lenses, and every morning you pick one. Once you do, you may not even be aware of how they color what you see throughout the day, but they do. In the same way, since we can't objectively see other people's hearts and intentions, we always view them through our own lenses. We can choose to look through a negative lens or a positive lens. It's a choice. In either case, our choice shapes how we see the world.

Presume positive intent. Even if you end up needing to confront the bad behavior, how much better will that conversation go if you enter into it assuming the best?

IDENTIFY THE SUBTITLES

Wouldn't it be great if interpersonal interactions came with subtitles? Instead of hearing what someone says and having to interpret its meaning and purpose, you would instead get to see live subtitles above everyone's heads explaining what they really meant.

Your supervisor calls you in and asks, "What do you think of your performance this quarter?" How do you respond? Are you about to get fired or promoted? Never fear, the subtitles tell you what she really means: "I'm really impressed with your leadership, and, if you sell me on yourself, I'm going to offer you the opportunity to supervise this project."

> **Our made-up subtitles become so real to us that we judge others by them.**

Wouldn't that be great? Wouldn't it save time and energy if we knew exactly what people meant and what the motives behind their actions were?

Sadly, no word yet from the tech world on when these ground-breaking subtitles will be available. In the meantime, we're left to interpret each other's intentions as best we can. As we do, we write our own subtitles, consciously or unconsciously, for what we think people are saying behind their words. Our made-up subtitles become so real to us that we start to judge others by them. And all too often, as we just discussed, our interpretations are wrong.

If we are going to have high-trust teams, we need to do two things:

First, we need to have the courage to share with others what subtitles we think they're communicating—especially when those subtitles are negative—and then seek clarity about whether our interpretations are correct. Give others the benefit of the doubt that they may not be.

Second, we need to do our best to provide our subtitles for the people we interact with by over-communicating our intentions and asking for feedback.

I recently met with an individual who was upset about the direction of his organization. He had moved to a new city with the belief that he would be part of the leadership team that would create and drive the new venture's vision. Well, a team was amassed, and he wasn't included. It seemed to him that the leader was controlling and that everyone around him was following like blind sheep. To his credit, he didn't believe the leader or any of the "sheep" had bad intentions, he just didn't approve of the direction. As you can imagine, he was frustrated. Not being involved like he had expected and seeing the direction of the organization go from what he had once imagined to something quite different was caus-ing great tension for him. His subtitles were making it impossible for him to operate out of high trust.

We talked about his and my versions of the subtitles that we thought were being communicated, and there was great variance between our two versions. He spent the next few weeks seeking clarity. He went to the leader and expressed his frustration. I asked him to take stock of his interpretations and feelings and to determine where he had ownership for what was going on. What was he causing? What was he participating in? And what was he allowing?

My friend is still living with some of these tensions, but he's moving towards seeking understanding. That isn't an easy road to travel, but when he started to take ownership for the subtitles, it seemed that the tide started to change and that his personal ownership increased.

Could incorrect subtitles be at the root of your team's trust gaps?

What kind of subtitles are you adding to your team members' words? What kind of subtitles do you think they add to yours? Could incorrect subtitles be at the root of some of your team's trust gaps? Pay special attention to this if there was a wide discrepancy in the responses to the Trust Factor assessment from one team member to the next; that can indicate that people are operating under different subtitles.

If you find yourself facing someone else's incorrect subtitles, make it your responsibility to correct the breakdown in communication. Make sure that message sent equals message received, and back up your words with actions that demonstrate your true intentions.

BE OFFENSIVE

One of the skills that will be helpful if your team members are to challenge their negative subtitles and assumptions about others (and one that is absolutely essential for high trust) is the ability to have healthy conflict.

Sometimes we can be too afraid of offending people. We want to keep things feeling good, so we avoid uncomfortable conversations and end up actually prolonging a bad situation. If we're going to have high trust, we need to be willing to be offensive.

Now, don't get me wrong; I'm not giving you permission to be disrespectful or harsh. But if you tend to avoid conflict, you should probably work on becoming more willing to offend people or make them uncomfortable when it's needed.

While destructive conflict is extremely hurtful, conflict doesn't have to be destructive. I want to make a plea to you to look for situations where conflict can actually build your relationships instead of tearing them down. If that idea sounds like a contradiction in terms, I would like to suggest a vocabulary change. When we're talking about conflict with others, let's distinguish between healthy conflict and unhealthy conflict.

In healthy conflict, there is disagreement, tension, or opposition, but it's not a personal attack. Everyone still believes the best about each other. You simply have a difference of opinion, which the conflict provides an opportunity to clarify and resolve. Healthy conflict leaves each party feeling heard and respected, builds empathy and trust, and equips you for a better relationship in the future. It's win/win for everyone.

Healthy conflict is win/win for everyone.

Unhealthy conflict, meanwhile, attacks your worth as a person. It's not just that the other person disagrees with your opinion, but that your opinion makes you suspect, ignorant, or less worthy of respect. Small disagreements reopen past frustrations that were never resolved. Emotions run high, and both parties lose sight of their common ground. You stop trying to see each other's point of view, and start merely trying to win. But this battle has no winners. Unhealthy conflict is lose/lose for all involved.

CANDOR WITH CARE

So how can we move our team towards having healthier conflict? Remember when we were talking about our responsibility in communication and the importance of making sure that message sent equals message received? In the midst of a conflict this becomes a hundred times more important.

When someone offends or disappoints us, or when we perceive negative subtitles beneath their words, the thing that determines whether that offense will lead to healthy or unhealthy conflict is the way that we communicate it.

And in case you're in doubt, the offense probably should be communicated. Not communicating it is almost a guarantee of unhealthy, passive-aggressive conflict. Keeping silent also doesn't give the person an opportunity to clear things up in case the offense is a misunderstanding.

If you had spinach in your teeth, would you rather someone tell you or let you continue as you were? Which is kinder? I would definitely want to be told! I think the same is true for interpersonal conflict. If you were unintentionally offending a coworker by continuing to speak carelessly about a sensitive topic, wouldn't you like to know it? It's more unkind to allow people to keep acting in a way that alienates others, and ultimately does a disservice to them, than it is to make them temporarily uncomfortable by addressing an offense.

But the *way* that you communicate an issue makes all the difference. If I were speaking to a group of people and one of them saw that my fly was down or that I had something hanging from my nose, I'd definitely want to know. But that doesn't mean I want a member of the audience to shout out in the middle of my talk, "Hey mister, zip it up!" A signal or note or quiet aside would do the job much better. We need to embrace conflict, but we also need to think before we speak and be wise about *how* we have conflict.

My company works with a client that has been teaching its employees the principles of lean manufacturing as they relate not only to production, operations, and logistics, but also to leadership. They teach their team members what it means to be lean leaders: to serve their employees, to eliminate waste from their human interactions, and to build the case for supporting and driving change. As part of that training, the president of one of their units coined the term "candor with care." He means that we must be willing to confront, challenge, and bring opposition with honesty and candor, but we must also do so with care.

To have candor with care:

- Affirm the ways that the person's behavior or working style can be a strength.

- Express your confidence in their good intentions.

- Avoid absolutes (always, never) in favor of more tentative language (sometimes, right now, in this situation).

- Avoid identity-targeted language (the way you are is bad) in favor of circumstantial and action-targeted language (your current actions are having a negative impact).

- Choose the right time and place to speak.

The chart below shows some specific examples of how the same behavior can be confronted in two different ways that lead to two very different outcomes. The statements on the left use candor only and lead to unhealthy conflict, while the statements on the right address the same situations with both candor and care, and lead to healthy conflict.

Back when I first started consulting, a client in the agribusiness industry said to me, "Richard, if you tell us what we want to hear, we're overpaying you." I took this advice to heart, and since that day I have vowed that I will do my best to tell people what they need to hear, not what they want to hear.

Conflict and confrontation may never be comfortable, but if your team members learn to do them well, they will be a deeper, richer team with high levels of trust—the kind of team that can weather any storm. It's all about learning the importance of our words.

CANDOR	CANDOR WITH CARE
You are arrogant and everyone is afraid of you.	I appreciate your self-confidence; it is one of your greatest strengths. When you overuse it, though, it can come across in a way that intimidates people.
You are too wishy-washy. People will never respect you.	You have a wonderful concern for others and a desire for unity. I think right now the team needs you to be bolder and to take a stand for what is important.
Getting a decision from you is like pulling teeth. You never decide anything until you've questioned every angle. Can't you just make a call already?	Your methodical approach usually helps you make good decisions. Right now, we need you to make a decision faster than you feel comfortable. How can I help you?
You obviously don't care about our working relationship, so I don't think it's worth my time to bother anymore.	I believe that you want us to have a strong working relationship, but I don't think you're aware how your actions sometimes undermine that. Can we talk?
Can you cut the sarcasm already? You're completely unprofessional.	I appreciate your sense of humor, and it's usually a fun dynamic in our staff. Lately, although I'm sure you don't mean it this way, I've felt embarrassed and attacked by it.
You are so close-minded. Stop hanging on to outdated traditions or get out of the way.	I appreciate that you value consistency and predictability, but I think that in this situation we should be more open to change. The environment around us is changing, and we must adapt with it or we'll lose the things we've worked so hard for.

WORDS ARE LIKE TOOTHPASTE

A CANDOR-WITH-CARE WORD PICTURE

Not too long ago I was trying to help my boys learn the lesson of the power of their words. I tried lecturing, I tried asking them to come up with new ways to describe their feelings, and I even tried role-playing. No luck.

Then one morning an idea came to me while I was brushing my teeth, a way to illustrate my point so that it would make a lasting impression. That evening I sat the two older boys down at the table and gave each of them a paper plate and a tube of toothpaste. I told them that they were going to have a race to see who could squeeze all the toothpaste out of their tube the fastest. With a "one, two, three!" they were off to the races. I don't remember who won, though I'm sure if you asked them they could tell you.

After the race was over, I told them that we would do one more race. This time, it was a race to see who could put the toothpaste back into the tube. With another "one, two, three!" they were off again, but not with as much gusto. This time the race wasn't as fun, and they weren't as successful.

With the smell of winterfresh toothpaste in the air and light blue stains on the boys' sticky hands, I looked in their eyes and said, "Boys, your words are like toothpaste. Once you let them out, you can't put them back in." I went on to add, "The tongue is like a sword, and has the strength and power to do big things. Be careful with the words you choose, because you can never take them back."

I've since used this illustration in rooms full of big-shot leaders in expensive suits, and the message hits home as well as it did with my boys. If we want high trust and healthy conflict, we must all take more care in the choice of our words.

GET OUT OF THE LOOP

As you examine the issues behind your team's gaps and encourage healthy conflict, be on the lookout for one issue that can run rampant in a low-trust team: gossip.

> **gos•sip: indirect, unhelpful conversations with someone other than the person who is responsible for or has the power to solve a problem**

You know what it means to be "in the loop." It used to be called water-cooler talk. It's when you understand all the social undercurrents, raised eyebrows, and whispers in the office. You're in the know. You know who's driving whom crazy, who is in, and who is out.

Who said middle school ended in eighth grade?

GOSSIP: A LOSE/LOSE SITUATION

Rumors and gossip may seem like small stuff, but they're like the tiny root that eventually breaks up a slab of concrete. They divide teams and push people apart. Gossip may make the "in" people feel even more "in" for a moment, but in the end it destroys unity and trust. It's the exact opposite of healthy, direct conflict, and it has no place in high-trust environments.

If one of your team members is having a problem with someone but goes and talks about it with a third party who doesn't have the authority or relationship to solve the problem, that is gossip. If a team member is complaining to a colleague about frustrations with their boss instead of speaking to the boss directly, that is gossip.

Gossip is unfair to every person involved. It is unfair to the person doing the gossiping because it damages other people's confidence in their integrity and compassion. It is unfair to the hearers because it puts them in an uncomfortable, unfair situation where they either have to call the gossiper out or passively support the gossip themselves. And it's definitely unfair to the person being gossiped about, because they are being shamed about a situation without any ability to address it head-on.

There are no innocent parties in the gossip loop. If people are in the loop they either actively participate in gossip or, at the very least, passively allow the gossip train to keep rolling. If you want a chance at high-trust relationships, you need to get out of the gossip loop, stay out of the gossip loop, and keep others out of the gossip loop.

Shutting Down the Gossip Loop

Here are a few strategies for how to shut down a gossip loop:

Walk away. When people start talking about others and it's not the right time to directly confront it, simply walk away.

Challenge it. Ask the parties involved if they are able to help solve the problem with this discussion. If not, say that while you're sure their intentions are good, it probably isn't in anyone's best interest to talk about other people's problems if they can't help solve them. They may be put off at first, but they should respect you.

Call it what it is. Let people know that they are participating in gossip and that it is harmful. Harmful to the parties being talked about and harmful to the parties doing the talking.

Give them options. Most times people who are gossiping would be best served by going directly to the people they are talking about. Give them the option to do so. If they won't do it, perhaps the other option is for you to bring it up on their behalf. Say something like, "I know you are frustrated with Kenny. I am going to see him next Thursday. I would suggest you talk to him by then. If you haven't, I am going to bring up your concerns and ask him to talk with you about them."

Make this a priority. Just don't gossip. It is tempting and sometimes feels like the right thing to do. Stop. Don't do it.

Apologize. If you have participated in gossip, apologize for doing so and let others know that you don't wish to participate in the conversation any longer. If you think it would be helpful, go to the person you were gossiping about, apologize, and seek their forgiveness.

Become part of the solution. In all of life's problems, you are either part of the problem or part of the solution. If gossip has made you part of the problem, then change that. Find a way to become part of the solution.

Turn your ears away. We all know when gossip is getting ready to happen. You can often tell by the way people are talking, their expressions, and the volume of their voices. When you hear this coming, turn your ears away. Don't lean in as a coconspirator. Choose not to participate.

Ask for help. Make it clear to your team members, family, and friends that you don't wish to perpetuate gossip. Share with them the definition of gossip and ask them to hold you accountable. When they do, don't get mad. Say thank you.

Pull the weed. Gossip is like a weed. You can mow over it and it will go away for a while, but until you get to the root and pull it out completely, the weeds will keep coming back. Figure out the root of gossip in your life. Are you a people pleaser? Do you want to be in the in crowd? Go to the root and pull it out.

Next time you're drawn to the water cooler, remember: get out of the loop.

A LOOK IN THE MIRROR

Once you've sought to understand your team's issues in the gaps that you see, it's time to look inward: What is *your issue* in them? How are you responsible for contributing to these gaps in trust?

Of all the tools and resources available to a leader, nothing beats an honest look in the mirror. There isn't a book or seminar that will give the kind of feedback and insight that you will get from examining yourself in the harsh light of day. Looking into the mirror requires you to accept responsibility that you are part of the problem and must be part of its solution.

A Self-Examination

In light of your team's Trust Factor results and the gaps that you found, ask yourself pointed questions like:

- How have my words or actions, or a lack of words or actions, contributed to this problem?
- Could I have miscommunicated my priorities?
- Have I pressured my employees to ignore problems for the sake of production?
- Do I accept feedback and criticism well?
- Do I have any insecurities as a leader that have kept me from intervening in this problem?
- Do I micromanage my team?
- Do I take time to know and develop my team members?
- How have I allowed a bad situation to continue?
- How well do I model the priorities and values I'd like to see in my team?

Before you can move on to plan solutions to your trust gaps, you need to face the mirror and do a thorough examination of yourself as a leader. Take responsibility for what you want to see changed.

Don't Forget Your Blind Spots

While you're looking in the mirror, don't forget that there's a lot about yourself that you can't see. When we drive a car, we know to check our blind spots. Some things are just too close for us to see clearly.

Life is the same way—we can't objectively see ourselves, so we need other people around us to show us our blind spots.

Do you have people in your life, trusted friends or mentors, whom you can ask for regular, honest feedback about how you can improve as a leader? If not, work on a short list of names and begin an ongoing discipline of asking for the hard-to-hear truth.

MAKE A GAME PLAN

THE ART OF TRUST

We've assessed your team, defined the gaps, examined the issues of others and self, and now it's time to make a game plan that will lead your team forward in continued development as a high-trust team.

With the information you've gained from the first three stages, it's time to come up with a plan for where to go from here.

> **Making your game plan requires faith, creativity, risk, and perseverance, much like trust itself.**

From here on, leading a team into trust is more of an art than an exact science. Your specific game plan needs to be tailored to the needs of your organization, because there is no single solution that fits every team. Making your game plan requires faith, creativity, risk, and perseverance, much like trust itself.

When I lead teams through the development of a game plan, I ask the following questions:

- How do you define what good looks like?

- How will you recognize it when you see it?

- What are specific ways that team members can hold each other accountable to that standard?

- What are three to five specific things your team can do that would have the greatest impact on increasing trust?

Over the next few pages, we'll look at each question in turn.

If you would like to speak with me or another Peak Solutions consultant about how to personalize this process to fit your team's specific needs, contact us and we'd be glad to help.

WHAT WOULD GOOD LOOK LIKE?

The first step in making your game plan is for your team to clarify, based on everything you've discovered up to this point, what "good" would look like. What would characterize your team if you loved coming to work, looked forward to working alongside each member of your team, and felt confident in your ability to overcome any obstacle?

You need to have a picture of the future you're aiming for. If you are so discouraged that you can't even envision what your team would look like with high trust, you'll never be able to achieve it. You have to see beyond today, beyond whatever unpleasant, unhealthy issues are tripping up your team, and believe that change can take place. You must have a vision of a better state than you are currently in.

Here are three questions that might help you define good for your team:

Does your team understand why they exist? Good would look like your team catching a vision for the larger purpose behind why they exist, what they are trying to do, what they hope to influence, and whom they are trying to serve. This is your highest goal. It's the reason that your people get up and come to work here on this team instead of all the other places they could work or all the other things they could do with their lives.

If you just trade money for time, people will give you time. But if they understand why they do what they do, they'll give you blood, sweat, and tears.

Does your team understand what they do? Good would look like your team having a clear picture of what role they play in the larger company, what the expectations are for their work, and exactly how their degree of success at their daily tasks helps or hinders the larger company from being successful, meeting their goals, and fulfilling their larger purpose.

How do you relate to each other? Good would look like relating to each other with mutual respect, engaging in healthy conflict and confrontation, challenging the problem instead of the person, and addressing offenses quickly instead of stuffing built-up emotion until it implodes.

Spend some time with your team brainstorming what good would look like for you.

HOW WILL YOU RECOGNIZE IT?

Once you know what you're aiming for, note the specific ways that your team will recognize progress when you see it along the way.

If you are navigating at sea, you don't just check your compass once, point your ship in the right direction, and then just hope that you hit land. You check and recheck your bearing, making sure you're aimed where you want to be, and noting signs of progress throughout the journey.

In the same way, you have to keep your definition of good in front of you so you know when you're meeting it or missing it, and can celebrate or recalibrate as needed. Take a minute now to talk about what it will look like for you to recognize that you are making progress towards your idea of good for your team.

Sometimes the signs along the way don't look like we expected. We say that we want open dialogue and healthy conflict, but when someone confronts us, we respond defensively. When we do that, we're effectively saying, "I know I said I wanted that, but I really didn't." That shows a lack of integrity and courage. Set the expectation that progress towards the goal of good will probably start out feeling uncomfortable.

As you take steps towards the good you're aiming for, plan regular times to look back at how far you've come and ahead at how far you still need to go. Call attention to your successes and make adjustments if you get off course.

HOW CAN THE TEAM HOLD ITSELF ACCOUNTABLE?

To make a high-trust team a reality, everyone must lead it. None of this works if the team relies on the leader to make it happen. No leader is strong enough to do that.

You will need everyone to take responsibility for leading and driving high trust if you want it to happen. Give your team members permission to give feedback in a way that maybe they haven't before. Set the expectation that people will call each other out when they see behavior that doesn't foster high trust.

Above the Line, Below the Line

Write a big line on your whiteboard. Above the line, write all the pro-trust behaviors or attitudes you can think of, like "ownership," "presume positive intent," and "welcome feedback." Below the line, write all the behaviors and attitudes that undermine trust, like "see people as adversaries," "blame," and "shift responsibility."

It should look something like this:

TRUSTWORTHY BEHAVIOR OWNERSHIP
WE FOCUS
WELCOME FEEDBACK DON'T TAKE OFFENSE
SEE PEOPLE AS ALLIES
RESPONSIBILITY PRESUME POSITIVE INTENT

SEE PEOPLE AS ADVERSARIES !
PERSONAL ATTACK ME FOCUS BLAME !
UNTRUSTWORTHY BEHAVIOR SHIFT RESPONSIBILITY
DEFENSIVE PRESUME NEGATIVE INTENT

Once you gain agreement on what behaviors are "above the line" and "below the line," this becomes the language team members can use to call each other out when someone does something that goes against your high-trust game plan.

One person can go to another, describe what they did, and say, "Do you think that was above the line or below the line? I see that behavior as below the line, and this is why. How can I help you act in a way that is above the line?"

Going Up Takes Everyone

I was facilitating a leadership development session one time when a man named Art, a retired army general and elementary school principle, stood up to illustrate a point. He asked another participant to climb on top of a stool and see if he could pull Art up to his level. The guy strained with everything in him, but Art's feet stayed firmly planted on the floor. Then Art said he was going to see if he could pull the other guy down. One light tug from the general and the guy was on the floor.

It's a lot easier to pull someone down to acting below the line than it is to pull someone up. It will require every member of your team to own and lead the transition to high trust if it is to happen. Get agreement now that you will all hold each other accountable and that each of you will welcome people calling you out when you fall short of pro-trust behavior.

It's hard to live above the line. Not safe, but good. Not easy, but worth it.

WHAT ACTIONS WOULD MAKE THE GREATEST IMPACT ON TRUST?

This is where it all comes together.

Sit together as a team and review your gaps and your picture of what good would look like. Now make a list of a few things that if you did them, and did them well, would have the greatest impact on closing your gaps and establishing higher trust.

For example, if one of your gaps was a mistrust of how the company manages its money, one of the things on your game plan might be to be more open with finances, such as by publishing a public budget each quarter. If one of your gaps was a lack of unity in the leadership team, you might plan to do something together as a team every month.

Other items that companies I've worked with have put on their game plan lists include:

- Communicate how each person's work impacts the bottom line.

- Deliver bad news as quick or quicker than good news.

- Help people know why they do what they do.

- Have shared experiences as a team.

- Allow more flexibility in the hours people work.

- Create a culture of candor.

Don't be limited by these examples. Look at your own situation and ask yourselves what few things, done right, would go the furthest towards building trust.

Once you have your list of action items, commit to doing putting them into practice and to holding each other accountable.

LEARN TO HATE
(THE STATUS QUO)

Now that you have the initial steps of your game plan, it's time to make change happen. But your team will only see change if they learn to hate—hate the status quo, that is.

Gleicher's formula says that change will occur when:

D x V x F > R

D = dissatisfaction with the current state of affairs

V = vision for how things could be

F = first steps, or practical ways to begin to achieve that vision

R = the resistance to change

Developed by David Gleicher and Richard Beckhard, this equation suggests that organizational change will only be successful when the product of D, V, and F is greater than the resistance to change. Because these three things are multiplied, if even one is missing or low there will not be enough momentum to overcome resistance.

But I want to take this a step further. A little dissatisfaction is not enough. We've perfected the art of being perpetually dissatisfied with a lot of things—our weight, our fitness, the time we spend with our kids, our friendships, etc.—without doing anything to change. You can't just wish things were different. You have to *hate* the way things are.

$$H \times V \times F > R$$

Hate What is Bad

Merriam-Webster defines hate this way:

hate: intense hostility and aversion, usually deriving from fear, anger, or a sense of injury

If you want to win higher trust, you and your team must learn to fear the idea of not changing. Become intensely hostile to the prospect of the next five years being the same as the last. Get a sense of injury about what a low-trust, self-protective, uncooperative environment costs you every day. Only then will you be sufficiently dissatisfied to make a change.

You can encourage H, hatred for the status quo, in your team by highlighting the cost of not changing. Have team members list the ways that your gaps affect morale, team turnover, productivity, creativity, pride in their work, and a feeling of mutual support within the team.

Cast a Vision for How Things Could Be

Next, communicate V: a vision for the future. What would it be like to work in a high-trust environment? How much easier would it be to communicate if team members always assumed the best about each other?

What would the wider ripple effects of change be? A more efficient team leads to a more successful business, which leads to greater opportunities and rewards for each of your team members. Working on a high-trust, high-performance team means more time in the "flow" of work, which is a proven predictor of happiness.

I've made plenty of resolutions to exercise more, but none stuck. Apparently the vision of me at the beach with the body of a twenty-five-year-old wasn't enough to motivate me. But you know what finally did it? I realized that if I didn't make a change, I wouldn't be able to hang with my kids as they grew up. I wanted to add life to my years and not be so tired, out of shape, and sloppy. When I started exercising for what it would do for my family instead of only for myself, I found the vision and fulfillment I needed to overcome my resistance. Keep your team's eyes fixed on whatever vision motivates them to push through their internal resistance and fight for change.

Determine Your First Steps

Finally, clearly outline F: the first steps to implement change. Break down big initiatives into small steps that can be started immediately.

Look at the action items that you put on your game plan. Are they able to be begun immediately? If not, break them down into smaller steps so that you can start the process without any more delays.

John Kotter, author of *Leading Change*, says that two key markers of success when managing change are the creation of a sense of urgency and the accumulation of small wins. Big, complex plans can be so intimidating that we don't even start. You don't have to achieve your end goal with the first step you take. The first step is just that–the first step. There will be more. You've heard the old adage about how to eat an elephant. This is the same: one bite (or step) at a time. Take that first step, then the second, and then keep on keepin' on.

Two key markers of success when managing change are the creation of a sense of urgency and the accumulation of small wins.

By deeply hating the status quo, getting a vision for what's possible, and laying out small first steps, you can overcome resistance, take ownership of your gaps, set your game plan in motion, and achieve lasting change.

MOTIVATION DOESN'T LAST

"People often say that motivation doesn't last. Well, neither does bathing. That's why we recommend it daily."
—Zig Zigler

One obstacle to organizational change is that it happens gradually, one step at a time, and requires as much focus, perseverance, and motivation on the hundredth day as on the first. Building and maintaining high trust is a marathon, not a sprint. Starting well is easy, but finishing well is even more important.

The problem with motivation is that people sit around waiting to be motivated by someone else. Motivation isn't an action that someone does to us; it's a state of being that we choose to continuously refresh, or not. We are motivated or we are not.

Motivation is like milk or cheese: it's fresh—for a while. If you are motivated to work on a Tuesday but wait until Friday to do it, your motivation will probably have worn off. Some people's motivation has a longer shelf life than others', but in the end, all motivation is perishable.

As a leader, you do not have the power to motivate others. I'm going to say that again. You do not have the power to motivate others. You can motivate exactly one person: *you.*

As my good friend and colleague Randy Boek says, the key to having a motivated team is "hire motivated people and don't do stupid stuff that demotivates them." You can't motivate people, but you can impact things that sap their motivation from them—like a draining environment, a limited vision of why their work matters in the big picture, micromanagement, and not celebrating their successes.

You can motivate exactly one person: you.

If you can allow people to find their own motivation and work in times and spaces that help them stay motivated, you will have a team of rock stars.

So how do we create an environment that helps sustain motivation and helps people find a purpose that drives and inspires them? This is different for every person, but here are a few ideas.

HELP THEM UNDERSTAND THE "WHY"

Embrace your new title as Chief Dot Connector. Research has shown that the greatest way to get discretionary effort from frontline employees is to show them how what they do impacts the overall strategy of the organization. Make sure they know why their job is important.

GIVE AUTHORITY AND GET OUT OF THE WAY

Allow your team members to solve problems. Give them tools and resources to do their job and let them be creative in how it gets done. Problems that get solved when and where they occur tend not to repeat themselves.

Any manufacturer hopes to eliminate defects from its products. In leadership, defects are not just confined to the physical production process. We have meeting defects, process defects, and people-interaction defects. Give each team member the authority to identify defects when they occur and to cut them out of the process.

REMIND THEM WHAT THEY'RE FIGHTING FOR

One of the best things you can do to help your people stay motivated is to understand their cause and remind them what it is. We all face battles each day, and our reasons for facing them are one of the most important things about us.

We face battles at work, from difficult coworkers to red-tape bureaucracy. We also carry with us silent personal burdens of sickness, the death of a loved one, divorce, bills, repairs, and problems with the kids.

Why do we bother fighting those battles? I can tell you my top five reasons:

1. Christy
2. Christian
3. Preston
4. Jackson
5. Lincoln

My reasons are my family—my wife and four boys. That cause is the most important thing about me. If I needed fresh motivation for a battle, I would just need to think about how failure or success would impact my family.

Do you know your team's causes? If not, find out what they are. Ask them about how their battles are going. Show how success at the battles you're asking them to face, whether it's the fight for high trust or a different battle, serves their causes.

Dwight D. Eisenhower once said, "Motivation is the art of getting people to do what you want them to do because they want to do it." To do this you must know their cause.

TAILOR THE REWARD TO THE PERSON

When you reward your team members for furthering high trust, succeeding at their jobs, or having years of service at your company, fit the reward to the person.

I once heard a story about how Disney learned this lesson the hard way. One of their employees was about to celebrate his fortieth anniversary working for the company. In an effort to recognize his many years of dedication, his supervisor arranged for a big party, complete with appearances by Mickey, Minnie, Goofy, and the whole crew. On the day of the party, about an hour before quitting time, they brought the employee to a big warehouse area. When he walked in Mickey jumped out of a cake, a band started playing, all his colleagues screamed "SURPRISE!" and confetti dropped from the ceiling. The party was a hit . . . or so they thought.

The next day, the man called in sick. His boss called and asked what was wrong. His reply was simply, "Don't ever do that again!"

Thankfully, the manager was smart enough to not get offended. He asked, "Well, what would you have preferred?"

The employee's response changed things at Disney forever. He said, "How about a phone call to my wife or my grown daughters thanking them for the sacrifices of my loyalty? Thanking them for the dance recitals, soccer games, and music programs that I missed over the years?"

Now, when Disney hires new employees, they say to them, "We know you will do things to exceed our expectations in the future. When you do, what would you prefer as a reward or incentive?" Then they offer a list of possible rewards, from gift cards, merchandise, and promotional opportunities to time off, training, and chances to serve on committees.

To create an environment that helps people stay motivated, don't reward people as you would like to be rewarded. Reward them as they would like to be rewarded.

TEST 'EM!

A great way to keep your team's motivation fresh is to give employees new challenges and job responsibilities. Too often, though, we're discouraged from doing this because we think of these new responsibilities as permanent changes to someone's job description. If they don't work out, we're kind of stuck. We can't very easily take a responsibility back without putting the person through a discouraging demotion, so we leave everyone's roles well enough alone. This is a shame, because offering new

> **Trust your people with small things, and if they do well, trust them with big things. Trust begets trust.**

opportunities can have such a positive impact on morale, motivation, trust, retention, and team member development.

Instead of making new responsibilities permanent, try giving a defined starting and ending time for the new role. Trust your people with small things, and if they do well, trust them with big things. Trust begets trust. Give clear expectations and let them know what level of authority they have for this new task.

That last part is key—too many leaders give people a project but forget to let them know how much authority they have. You can pick the most appropriate level of authority for a given situation

- Level 1: Act when directed
- Level 2: Act after approval
- Level 3: Act after consultation
- Level 4: Act and report
- Level 5: Act autonomously

Give your team member a test, and, if they pass it, give them another one. This way, they're encouraged to stay motivated, you get to test how they do in the new role, and trust goes up.

LEAD STRONG

"People are doing the best that they can. They will do better when they know how. It is our job to help them know how."
–Randy Boek

Congratulations—you have started the journey of leading a high-trust team. You understand that trust is given, not earned. You know how to increase trust by building confidence in integrity, competence, and compassion. You've assessed your team, defined the gaps, examined the issues, and made your game plan. Great job. You have a big vision for your team. To see it become reality, you will have to lead strong.

Our culture hasn't done a great job at providing models of strong leadership (or, for that matter, of what it looks like to be a healthy follower). It's not about autocracy, control, rules, or compliance. Authority is not meant to inhibit people, but to help them flourish. Mature, intelligent people put themselves under authority because it helps them thrive.

People are dying to be led. They don't want to be controlled and micromanaged, but they do want to be led. When I ask my clients about the difference between horrible bosses and great bosses, the energy in the room changes from night to day. The horrible bosses are controlling, directing, absent, and hypocritical. They don't support their teams, they steal their ideas, and they are more focused on protecting their turf than their team. The great bosses are encouragers who set high standards and challenge people to reach their potential. They give feedback, both good and bad, and are relentless in developing their people. Be a great boss.

Leading your team well is a higher priority than anything else that you do. Be an intentional leader. If your team is not where you want them to be right now, don't get frustrated with them. Make it your job to show them a better way.

As in all things, trust starts with you. As we said in the first pages of this book, the ten most powerful two-letter words in the English language are *if it is to be, it is up to me.* Above-the-line, high-trust behavior starts with you.

Lay down your rights. Take responsibility. Get creative. Stay patient. Lead strong.

Acknowledgments

First off, to the jerks and challengers, the naysayers and sabo-
teurs, thank you! We have all experienced people who have been
slow to trust, difficult to deal with, or scarred from past betrayal.
Without these difficult situations, I would not have had to rethink
my approach to trust. You helped to shape these ideas, and for that
I am extremely grateful.

To my clients and colleagues, I feel blessed to do what I love
and what God created me to do. Thank you for the platform to
bring out the best in you and to be challenged to do the same in
myself. Every day of work is an opportunity to make a difference in
the world and in your lives.

Kevin Freund, here it is, finally. Thanks for asking, and asking,
and asking.

To my editor, Laura Tucker, you helped me find my voice and
gave me the confidence to complete this book. This book has been
in me for over a decade and you helped to bring it out. Thank you
for pushing and for caring.

To all my friends, thanks for your support and encouragement.

Jake, you've heard all my stories, served as a sounding board
and continue to make the Peak Solutions experience magical.

Grant, thanks for serving me and believing in me and pointing
me back home. "Come on now, let's do this."

To my dad who has always said "Yes you can" and to my mom
who has said "If it's worth doing, it's worth doing right," your
wisdom and love are amazing.

To my wife Christy, you have held down the fort and carried the
burden during endless travel and years of service to our amazing clients. Our kids are a great reflection of your love and your

willingness to give trust. You helped guide and shape this project, and nothing would have been possible without your vision and feedback. You are my best friend and I love my life with you.

To my boys, Christian, Preston, Jackson, and Lincoln, I love being your dad and pray that you will be men of courage, passion, and honor. Be willing to trust. It may not be safe, but it's good.

Holy Spirit, thank you for your guidance, your truth, and your relationship. Thank you for sending Jesus to show us the ultimate example of trust.

ABOUT THE AUTHOR

Richard Fagerlin is an author, an organizational development consultant, and a professional speaker. As the president of Peak Solutions, Inc., a management consulting firm, Richard works with CEOs, leadership teams, and midlevel managers to develop leadership skills and help them achieve alignment throughout their organizations. His client list includes global giants, pillars of local communities, and everything in between.

Richard lives in Fort Collins, Colorado with his wife and four boys. When not working, he enjoys running, skiing, cycling, and any kind of adventure with his family. One day he hopes to be half the man his kids think he is.

For more information about Peak Solutions, please visit www.peaksol.com

FOR MORE INFORMATION ON
HOW TO PUT THESE PRINCIPLES INTO ACTION

PLEASE CONTACT
a Peak Solutions consultant at:
peaksol.com

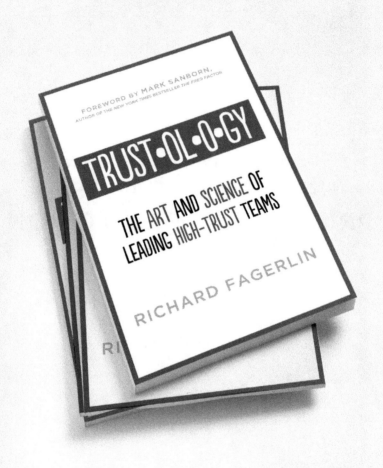

FOR BULK DISCOUNTS & CUSTOMIZED ORDERS
please contact: *sales@wiseguyspress.com*

CPSIA information can be obtained
at www.ICGtesting.com
Printed in the USA
FFHW01n0915290618
47274777-50194FF